Another Day in Showbiz

Another Day in Showbiz

by

PIERRE COSSETTE

ECW PRESS

Published by ECW PRESS
2120 Queen Street East, Suite 200, Toronto, Ontario, Canada M4E 1E2

NATIONAL LIBRARY OF CANADA CATALOGUING IN PUBLICATION DATA

Cossette, Pierre, 1923-
Another day in showbiz: one producer's journey / Pierre Cossette

ISBN 1-55022-557-X

1. Grammy Awards. 2. Cossette, Pierre, 1923- . I. Title.

ML76.G7C83   2003   781.64'079'73   C2002-905101-0

Copy editor: Mary Williams
Cover design: Guylaine Regimbald – SOLO DESIGN
Typesetting: Yolande Martel
Production: Emma McKay

Cover illustration: © Al Hirschfeld. Art reproduced by special arrangement with Hirschfeld's exclusive representative, The Margo Feiden Galleries Ltd., New York. Photographs: All uncredited photos appear courtesy of Cossette Productions. Diligent efforts have been made to contact copyright holders; please excuse any inadvertent errors or omissions. The publisher would be pleased to receive notification and to make acknowledgments in future printings.

Printing: Transcontinental

This book is set in Sabon and Caflisch

The publication of *Another Day in Showbiz* has been generously supported by the Canada Council, the Ontario Arts Council, and the Government of Canada through the Book Publishing Industry Development Program. **Canadä**

DISTRIBUTION

CANADA: Jaguar Book Group, 100 Armstrong Avenue, Georgetown, Ontario L7G 5S4

UNITED STATES: Independent Publishers Group, 814 North Franklin Street, Chicago, Illinois 60610

EUROPE: Turnaround Publisher Services, Unit 3, Olympia Trading Estate, Coburg Road, Wood Green, London N22 6T2

AUSTRALIA AND NEW ZEALAND: Wakefield Press, 1 The Parade West (Box 2266), Kent Town, South Australia 5071

PRINTED AND BOUND IN CANADA

ECW PRESS
ecwpress.com

*I dedicate this book to Foopie, Johnny, Andy, and Five—
and to my former boss and all-time idol, Lew Wasserman.*

Acknowledgments

IN THE ALMOST FIVE DECADES I have been in show business, I owe much to many. I could not have completed this book were it not for the parade of stars, celebrities, and public figures whose stories make up the bulk of what you are about to read. I am indebted to them and to the many, many friends I have made working in this business I love so much. It was my wife, Mary, Mother of Five, who encouraged me to turn what had been a collection of interviews and disjointed stories into something resembling the book you are now holding in your hands. Her support, her wonderful humor, and her faith in me are traits I've come to rely on and seldom thank her for. Thank you, Five.

Contents

Foreword

HE'S HUNCHED in the thirtieth row of the massive Staples Center, far away from the cardboard cutouts indicating where Britney Spears, Justin Timberlake, U2, and Céline Dion will be sitting for the Forty-Fourth Annual Grammy Awards in a few nights. He's careful to stay out of the way of the wiggy OutKast crew, who are about to take the stage for rehearsal, as well as the thousand-man-strong army still busily assembling sets and moving equipment. Sporting a cap, nondesigner sweatpants, and sneakers and flashing an ear-to-ear beam, he looks like an oversized teddy bear, perhaps the grandfather of a performer. Appearances can be awfully deceiving. In fact, this unassuming septuagenarian, Pierre Cossette, is a grandfather, but to all the techs and musicians in the arena he is far better known as the Father of the Grammys.

It was back in 1969 when this native of the small, rural Canadian town of Valleyfield, Quebec, first approached the National Academy of Recording Arts and Sciences and asked to purchase the rights to televise the Grammy Awards. After much wrangling and hair-pulling, Cossette got his wish two years later and produced the Grammys live for the first time on the tube.

Prior to Cossette's involvement, the Grammy Awards were presented in a hotel before a small audience, generally consisting of a few performers and their families. Times change. For this year's show, more than fourteen thousand people will fill the Staples Center, and an estimated one billion TV viewers will scope the gyrations of virtually every star in the business. And those stars who aren't appearing in the telecast will likely be in the audience. Few have to be coerced, for the Grammys are to the music biz what the Oscars are to the movie biz.

Watching the proceedings from his seat in the Staples Center, Cossette says softly, "It all starts with a desk, a telephone, and a wastebasket, and then it mushrooms into the single largest entertainment production on television." Even in Hollywood, who could have believed that such a fairytale could be possible?

—Bill Brownstein, at the Grammy Awards in Los Angeles
February 2002

Preface

ON MARCH 21, 1994, I found myself sitting fourth row center at the Sixty-Sixth Annual Academy Awards, surrounded by Oscar nominees. Steven Spielberg was four seats away, and Tom Cruise sat directly in front of me. Although for the past twenty years I had watched the telecast at Irving "Swifty" Lazar's famous Oscars parties, held at Spago, this was my first live attendance at the event. It was almost as thrilling as the night in 1995 when I was honored by the National Academy of Recording Arts and Sciences for having initiated the annual live televising of the Grammy Awards in 1971. On both occasions, I thought to myself, "How did I get here?"

So, how did I get from my inauspicious beginnings in the small town of Valleyfield, Quebec, Canada to where I am now? I'm successful and happy, finally; I'm lucky enough to have found my true calling early in life and smart enough to have pursued it relentlessly; and I'm fortunate enough to have made two wonderful marriages and produced two wonderful sons.

For someone whose entire life has been show business, it seems serendipitous that the house in which I was born, on December 15, 1923, should now be a restaurant called Club Touriste. Although I was five when I left, when I revisited at the age of fifty I experienced an unbelievable rush as I stood inside, at the staircase. What the actual events that occurred there were, I'll never know. All I was left with was that enormous physical sensation that I suspect must be what keeps addicts hooked.

A Kid from Canada

THIS COULD BE the most unlikely Hollywood success story you'll ever read. Frankly, there was precious little in the cards to indicate that someone with such an inauspicious start in life as mine would amount to much.

Let's backtrack—a lot. It was 1928 when my family picked up and left the tiny hamlet of Valleyfield, Quebec, Canada and moved to the land of milk and honey that is, apparently, California. I was all of five at the time, just barely out of diapers and no one's notion of worldly. My memories are, naturally, rather fuzzy. Oddly, or perhaps sadly, about all I do recall is my friend Jackie Chisholm and I showing off our private parts, as five year olds are wont to do. Except I don't think most kids' dads react like mine did. He caught me in the act and dragged me inside. He put a pair of pliers in the oven. In a few minutes he grabbed a potholder and took out the pliers saying that if he ever caught me doing that again he'd cut my pee-pee off. He was the one who brought up the story years later, asking me if I remembered the incident. Well, yeah—how could a kid forget a thing like that?

I also remember the sort of euphoric experience that boys have, if they're lucky enough, when they hide out and try to catch a girl undress by a window. The girl in my case was Jackie's aunt. We watched her strip naked and, as little as we were, we went absolutely crazy. Again we were caught—this time by Jackie's sister.

Sorry—not the stuff of greatness. But wait, there was one more telling childhood memory, maybe one of those inexplicable things that actually sent me into show business. When I was about seven years old, I was living with my mother, my father, and my sister on Garfield Avenue in Pasadena—the place where I grew up. An old man lived next door. A ventriloquist, he would talk to a clump of bushes alongside our driveway, saying things like, "Hey, what are you doing in there?" And out of the bushes would come the answer: "I'm not doing anything. What are you doing?"

Many decades later, as I was showing my wife my Garfield Avenue home, I walked over to those bushes, still believing there was somebody in there. Intellectually, I knew it wasn't so, but the kid in me couldn't let go of the idea that a real person was lurking there. I told my wife that at that time the Lindbergh case had all parents fearing for their children. They believed that if it could happen to the high and mighty, the people who could afford all the protection in the world, then no one was safe.

Those were the Great Depression years. My father lost his job at a lumber company, and all I remember seeing him do was cry. I was stunned, and I told him what adults always tell their kids: "Don't worry. Everything's going to be okay." There and then, I knew I had to do something to avoid a similar fate.

Eventually, my dad did manage to land a job at a Sears Roebuck store. Soon after, he stole a bicycle from the store for me. My mother was livid: "How could you do such a thing?" They had a huge fight. My father kept shouting that I was his kid and he wanted me to have a bicycle. Whether it was the hard times or their basic incompatibility, I don't know—maybe it was a little of both—but it had become obvious to me that they had little, if anything, in common and that they were both pretty miserable.

Although I was unaware of it then, my mother saw my father as a playboy with a major drinking problem. As a kid, I would listen to her putting him down mercilessly in ways I couldn't forgive. But, instead of developing a fierce loyalty to my father in the face of this, I grew more and more ashamed of him—my mother prevailed.

When I was an adolescent, for some reason I fell in with the rich kids in town. At that point, I was acutely embarrassed when my father, now working in a gas station, would show up wearing his uniform, announcing to the world that he was "just a working stiff"—something my mother never failed to show her contempt for. It was years before I was able to get past all that.

One of the anomalies of my young life came about when my grandfather died and left money to my mother. She bought a small apartment house near the junior high school I attended and, from that time on, we went to Canada every other summer. My father was still working in the gas station, so the neighbors couldn't figure out how we could afford to "summer in Canada." One summer, a friend of mine told his mother I was leaving again for Canada, and I remember her commenting, sarcastically, "I wish my husband worked in a gas station." In fact, when my mother inherited that money, my father had a brainstorm: Why not open a car wash on the Las Vegas Strip? My mother, of course, gave that idea a resounding no. He could have been a millionaire if she had agreed to that move. That just about summed up his life.

Clearly, the memories I have of my father are tangled—warm memories reside next to wretched ones. As a kid, I really wasn't aware that I was always looking for something from him. I remember like it was yesterday when he got the day off to come and watch me in a track meet. I was a super athlete in high school; I even made city champion. I was so nervous having him there that in my zeal to perform I hit a hurdle. Even though that put me in second place, I still qualified for the finals, in which eight schools were competing. I was used to running the 120-yard low hurdles, but now the coach was also asking me to run the 220 (a nonhurdle event). I ran it wide open from the gun to the finish line. I remember at the end feeling as if I was walking through molasses. But I won. I vividly recall the rare look of joy on my dad's face when I hit the finish line. For once, someone was proud of me.

Some years later, as a young GI, I was on a train pulling into the Pasadena station, returning home from the war. I hadn't told my parents I was coming that day. Looking out the window, I was astonished to see my father in his gas station uniform. He didn't see me. "Wow!" I thought. "How in God's name did he know I was coming in?" I was very excited. I got off the train and looked around for him. I watched him approach quickly and walk right past me to an attractive woman who had got off the train ahead of me. They hugged and kissed. I stood there, frozen. My mother was always telling me that he was having affairs with other women, but I hadn't believed it. I told my mother about the incident and urged her to get a divorce. It created serious tension between my dad and me. He blamed me for breaking up his marriage; but in the end he did marry the girl from the railway station, and life changed for him. His new wife had some money, apparently, and they leased a ramshackle, twelve-room hotel and bar in Eureka. They built it into a good business and were later able to buy a bar and restaurant in Long Beach and, soon after that, a beautiful home.

My mother was a gifted musician. I have kept the various awards she received in her lifetime. For some reason, and I do regret it, I never asked her to teach me how to play piano. She probably passed her "performance" genes on to me in a mutated form, but even years later, when I had achieved some success in the business, she would say, "Of all the cousins, the nephews, and the nieces, you're the only one in the family who has no talent." She attributed my accomplishments in show business to luck.

It has taken me years to develop my own philosophy of talent. To me, playing the piano is one kind of talent; pulling yourself up by the bootstraps in the face of adversity is another. And the sweet old African-American lady in Chicago who turned around all those kids who weren't cutting it in school and saw a lot of them make it into Harvard, that's talent. I firmly believe that when we're born, we are goodness, and from then on some of us are fortunate enough to hold on to it while others go down that road for a little while and then take a wrong turn.

My father died at the age of sixty-three. When he died, I cried like a baby. Then I realized that I knew practically nothing about him. I couldn't say whether he was a conservative or a liberal, a Democrat or a Republican. I had no sense of what his thoughts were on religion, or education, or the world in general. I had all those years to find out more about him, and I didn't do it. Now it's too late, and I carry that with me.

As for my mother, years before she died, I remember her saying over and over, "I can't wait to die. I can't wait to die." When she did go, I was embarrassed by my feelings, which were more of joy than sorrow. "She's happy now, at least," I thought to myself. I didn't go to the burial site to see the coffin lowered into the ground, but not because of my angry feelings towards her. I just find it voyeuristic to stand around and watch someone be placed in the ground in a box. I emerged from childhood with a grim view of family life. Fortunately, that view changed in later years.

Sometimes I say to myself, "Why do you put down your mother and father? Why do you say that your childhood was so unhappy? After all, you turned out okay. So what damage did they do to you?" Well, I have no good answers. My sister would be surprised to hear me complain about my childhood. She would insist that we had a wonderful upbringing. But she and I couldn't be more different, and all the kids we went to school with would confirm that. She was as quiet as I was flamboyant. To me, she seemed very innocent, very sheltered. She's someone who, if a nuclear bomb exploded (and she was still standing), would say, "Isn't that beautiful!" while everyone else was diving for cover.

In 1984, when I was living in the first Malibu home I ever owned, on La Costa Beach, my sister came to visit. She was always convinced that I could have been a successful doctor or lawyer; she didn't see show business in the same light. To let her know how well I was doing without making a big deal of it, I took what I thought was a subtle approach. I had purchased the house after I had seen it featured in *Unique Homes*, a real estate publication featuring top-end houses. I showed her the magazine with the picture of my house and said, "Here. This is how I found this house." I assumed she would notice the price, which was $1,695,000. She glanced at it and said, "You paid $169,000 for this place?" I didn't know how to answer. I couldn't bring myself to say, "No, I paid one million six hundred and ninety-five thousand dollars for it." That's my sister.

So, my sister has her childhood memories, and I have mine. My mother affectionately called me her "petit chou-chou" (her little cabbage), but it never made up for the fact that she was never there for me when I needed her. There was a time, in the mid-fifties, when I was starting my own business and badly needed capital. Knowing she had inherited fifty thousand dollars, I asked to borrow ten thousand. She made up some cockamamie excuse for refusing. No amount of pleading would move her. I ended up borrowing it from my secretary, Phyllis Jaffe. To this day, I am grateful to Phyllis, who could have had a job for life with me if she'd wanted it.

In the end, though, it was my parents' constant fighting that left the strongest mark on me. Early on, I vowed that my relationship with my kids was not going to be anything like the one I had with my mother and father. I was going to turn that around. And I think I did manage to do that.

One positive thing that I attribute to my childhood experiences, although it's probably innate, is my deep attraction to water. My place in Canada is on the St. Lawrence River, my place in New York overlooks the Hudson, and in California we live by the sea. I feel deeply connected to the sea. I can easily fantasize about having evolved from plankton to amoeba to a critter that swam, crawled, walked, and flew. I feel that I have been all those creatures and that when I die I will relive the process.

One of the more mundane things I realized about myself as the years went by was how important it was, and still is, that people like me or love me. I really don't care that much about money. Sure, I like being acknowledged by people in the business, but when I walk down the street in Hollywood no one knows my name, and that's okay with me. I take great satisfaction in putting on benefits to raise money for worthy causes, but I know in my heart that what I get from it is the sense that people care about me. It's a big part of what I get out of doing everything I do.

Showbiz Roots

LET THE RECORD SHOW: my first showbiz venture was getting Red Skelton to do a show at my high school in Pasadena. How did I get Red Skelton? Piece of cake. One day, I was walking across Colorado Boulevard, in front of the school. Robert Taylor, driving a convertible, came to a stop next to me. I looked straight at him. He waved hello, and I waved back. From that point on, I felt that the stars I had once considered beyond human reach were real people. So I got on the phone and called MGM. Fifty or sixty calls later, I'd nailed Skelton. My career as a theatrical entrepreneur was launched.

My confidence also came from the fact that I was always a top performer in the IQ tests we were given during my post-high-school stint in the army. In other words, I knew I had the brains to do it and that it was just a matter of will and hard work.

When the war was over, I went to Pasadena Junior College on the GI Bill; I wanted to complete the high school curriculum so I could transfer to the University of Southern California. I studied day and night. I don't think I left the house more than ten times that year. I never worked so hard in my life. I managed to get into USC on a special trial. In my first semester, I pulled down As and Bs. I attended school year-round so I could finish in three years instead of four. And I made it. I still get a tremendous kick out of saying, "I graduated from USC."

One of the classes I had taken at USC was in radio and television. In it, I learned about sound—very useful for a producer. I had access to all the sound effects material they had on file, and I used that material to pull a stunt that would set the stage for one I was to pull many years later. Another student had presented his radio audition tape, and it included a multiple-car-crash scene. The sound effects he used were incredible. As I listened, an idea formed in my young and fertile mind. I commandeered the crash tape and brought it back to the Phi Delta Theta House, where I was living. Then I persuaded an electrical engineering student to be my partner in mounting a frat-row "happening." Within a week, we had planted eight-inch speakers on every telephone pole and high point along frat row. We wired the speakers to a tape player in Phi Delta Theta House. At precisely 4:00 a.m., beside ourselves with anticipation, we put on the crash sound effects tape and pushed the button. The sound of a blood-curdling crash, followed by the screech of skidding tires, then another crash, carried far beyond frat row. The noise could be heard for blocks around. Hundreds of pajama-clad people were soon roaming the streets. Fire engines and police cars were all over the place. No one could locate the exact crash site, neither could they find the wreckage. News travels fast, however, and, the next day we were busted. We hadn't really thought about the consequences. Thank God, no one in the "madding crowd" had been injured. If so, we'd have been in real trouble.

My real start as a producer came in 1949, when I graduated from USC. By then, I owned *Campus* magazine, an independent, private publication distributed to sixty colleges around the country. *Campus* was the main competition for *Wampus* magazine, owned by USC and edited by students in the journalism department. The editor of *Wampus* was the now-famous Art Buchwald; the publisher was the equally well-known David Wolper. Just before graduation, I realized that if I was to see *Campus* succeed as an independent venture I would have to raise a considerable amount of money. There would be no more unpaid student labor to turn out the editorials, photos, ad layouts, sports and entertainment features, and news reports, not to mention secretarial and sales services. I had to raise money fast, or the whole thing would fall apart.

I went from door to door in downtown L.A. selling ads, but my first sacrifice was to sell my Ford to produce some working capital. As little as that netted me, it did allow me to stage "the *Campus* Magazine All-College Jamboree" at the Hollywood Palladium. Fortunately, *Campus* had a radio column, a television column, a motion picture column, and a built-in college readership. That gave me a way to get to the stars and elicit their help to put on a show. And that I did. The turnout was fabulous: the event drew one of the three largest audiences in the history of the Palladium. It was certainly a coup, but there was a major glitch to deal with before we could pull it off.

Three days before the show, I got a call from I.B. Kornblum, the head of the Theater Authority, the organization that controlled the activities of the various unions of performing artists. He told me that only certain charitable organizations (the Red Cross and four others) were allowed to pay performers at minimum union scale. He asked me which of the five was receiving the profits from the show. Innocently, I replied, "I'm doing this for *Campus* magazine. The proceeds will allow me to continue the magazine after I graduate."

"You can't do that," Kornblum said. "You're going to have to pay the artists their normal fees." I had managed to book such luminaries as Jack Benny, Bing Crosby, George Burns, and Phil Harris, so I answered, "Normal fees? I have fifteen of the biggest stars in show business. How can I pay them their normal fees?" We settled the dispute the day before the show. All income would accrue to the stars. I could deduct only the direct expenses I incurred. It was the first of many lessons I was to learn.

In the course of putting this show together, I had contacted several agents and agencies around town. The biggie at the time was Music Corporation of America, better known as MCA. On the strength of the show's success, MCA, after several meetings, offered me the job of booking shows on the college circuit, a very hot market at the time. I took it. My first assignment was to hit the road for two months, first with Harry James and His Orchestra, next with Bob Wills and the Texas Playboys, and then, for a week, with Jack Benny, Martin and Lewis, and Spike Jones. I was supposed to book band and concert dates, especially on college campuses.

By the time I came back from these tours, I had gained enough experience to feel like a real agent. Not bad for a kid just out of college. At this time, the early fifties, college dates were the only major money dates left in the big band business. My predecessor, I found out, was an old vaudeville-type booker who had little if any knowledge of the college scene. Soon I was the wonder boy of MCA. I quadrupled the MCA college business that first year, and what a training program it was working with Tommy Dorsey, Benny Goodman, and all the big-name bands of the era! I'd always wanted to be a drummer—I had a set of makeshift drums when I was a teenager and drove my dad crazy playing them all the time—so you can imagine how thrilled I was to book Harry James and His Orchestra for MCA. Harry would let me sit in on drums during the band's warm-up. I would sit at Louis Bellson's drums behind equally famous sidemen. It was a thrill beyond description.

But I almost lost my job over what I thought was a terrific scheme. I had booked Harry James and His Orchestra into the San Diego Ballroom on a Saturday night. The band usually went on at 8:00 p.m. and started warming up twenty minutes before that. But this night, I planned something special. The contract I gave Harry indicated an 8:00 p.m. start time, but the actual booking was for 9:00 p.m. This maneuver allowed me an hour-long warm-up with this great band. Three or four of the musicians were in on it, but I hadn't counted on Harry starting to panic when, by 8:30 on a Saturday night in one of America's foremost ballrooms, hardly anyone had shown up to see him. What else could he think but that his career was going into the dumper? Fortunately, he kept his cool. By 9:30, the place was jammed to the rafters. Harry found out what I had done, and he was really pissed about it. A few months later, however, it had become one of his favorite stories.

I was surprised one day when MCA president Lew Wasserman called me into his office and said I was doing a sensational job and was due for a promotion. "Wow!" I said to myself. "Maybe I'll be transferred to the motion picture or television department." Not likely. Lew wanted to send me on a three-month trip across the U.S.A. to visit every major nightclub and meet the stars. What I didn't know about show business when I set out on this trip, I learned in the course of it.

It was not until I returned that I found out what Lew's plan was. MCA had to have someone covering Vegas bookings. Apparently, Lew decided that the bosses wouldn't know what to make of this fresh young kid with his dimples, his big laugh, his infectious personality, and his tenacity. He figured that by making me head honcho not only of Las Vegas but also of Reno and Tahoe, he'd throw those guys so off guard they wouldn't know how to handle it. So, there I was, not more than a year out of college, heading for Las Vegas to meet the casino bosses of the five hotels that had given the city its reputation: the Flamingo, El Rancho, Thunderbird, Desert Inn, and Last Frontier. (They were actually the only hotels in Las Vegas at that time.)

Of course, those bosses laughed, every one of them, when I introduced myself as MCA's man in charge of talent for Las Vegas. At first they thought I was kidding. When I persisted, they got Lew on the phone and said, "Are you crazy? Sending a schoolboy up here to do business!" But what could they do about it? In my pocket I carried a list of MCA clients that could have subbed for a who's who of show business. All the superstars of the day were on that list: Frank Sinatra, Lena Horne, Nat King Cole, Bing Crosby, Joe E. Lewis, Judy Garland, Martin and Lewis. And every hotel wanted them.

One night at the Flamingo, I was sitting near boss Gus Greenbaum. It was opening night, and I had booked the entire show: the Fanelli Chimps, Dave Barry, and Tony Martin. The first show ran seven minutes too long. As soon as it ended, Greenbaum called me over and said, "I want a one-hour-and-fifteen-minute show. This one ran one hour and twenty-two minutes. If the second show goes over one hour and fifteen, I'm gonna break your fuckin' legs." He said it, and I knew he meant it. Gus was tough. (They found him a couple of years later with his throat slashed.)

Needless to say, I panicked. I went to Tony Martin, explained my problem, and asked him if he could cut three or four minutes from his act. "I'll get Dave Barry to cut the rest," I said. Tony Martin said, "Hey, get him to cut the whole seven minutes. He was on too long anyway." I went to Barry, who said, "What? I didn't even have time to get warmed up. Okay—for you, I'll cut three and a half minutes, but you owe me, big time." So I approached the monkey act. An Italian who spoke no English headed the Fanelli Chimps. Through a translator, he explained that the monkeys only knew the act from beginning to end; they couldn't be made to start in the middle of their music.

Now I was really panicking. Just before show time, I spoke to Eddie Fitzpatrick, the orchestra leader, and I asked him if he could start the music for the monkey act three and a half minutes before the curtain went up. The monkeys could start their routine and the curtain would go up three and a half minutes into their act and everything would be fine.

Sitting next to Greenbaum—he'd insisted on it—I felt emotionally drained. The show was to begin at 11:00 p.m. At 10:56 and thirty seconds, the monkey music started behind the curtain. It sounded like perfect background music. Backstage, the monkeys were rolling their baby carriages and carrying on with their act. At 11:00, a voice-over announced: "Ladies and gentlemen, the Flamingo Hotel is proud to present the Fanelli Chimps, comedian Dave Barry, and the star of our show, Tony Martin! And now, the Fanelli Chimps!"

The curtain went up to reveal ten monkeys flying in every possible direction, doing unbelievable acrobatics, building up to their big finish. People looked up, startled; they were putting their dessert spoons up their noses instead of in their mouths. The fanfare came to a climax, and the monkey act went off to big applause. The show went on, and it was over in exactly one hour and fifteen minutes. Gus Greenbaum, delivering a rare compliment, said, "You done good, kid. But the fuckin' monkey act was too long."

It was during that first year I spent at MCA that Lew Wasserman called me and said, "Pierre, do you speak French?"

With a name like mine, what could I say but "Yes, sir."

He said, "Can you be at the screening room downstairs tonight at 7:00?"

Again, I said, "Yes, sir."

He said, "I'll meet you there. Wear a suit and tie."

When I hung up, I asked myself why I'd told him I could speak French. I can speak it better than most Americans can, but I'm a long way from fluent.

Still confused, I showed up at 7:00 p.m. I gulped as I saw several people coming towards me from the executive dining room, which was adjacent to the screening room. First came Clark Gable, then Wasserman, then Alfred Hitchcock, and then Jimmy Stewart. Lew took me aside and said, "Mr. Hitchcock is trying to get Mr. Gable and Mr. Stewart to do a movie that was originally done in French a few years ago. There are no subtitles, so we'll need you to translate as we go along."

Everyone took a seat in the screening room, and Lew said, "Gentlemen, we have a young man here, Pierre Cossette, who will interpret for us as we go along. Pierre, say hello to Mr. Gable, Mr. Stewart, and Mr. Hitchcock." My stomach was lodged in my throat as the lights went down and the screen lit up. In the first three minutes there was virtually no dialogue—it was all cinematic setup of the story. Then came the dialogue. I did not understand one single word of it. I saw my promising career in show business going down the drain. After a while, Lew turned to me and said, "Pierre, what are they saying?" I gulped some more and said nothing. I was sweating bullets. Suddenly, mercifully, up pipes Alfred Hitchcock, explaining word by word what had happened up to that point in the movie. What Lew didn't know was that Hitchcock spoke fluent French. Alfred Hitchcock saved a young man's ass that day. I found out later that he told a mutual friend, "That new kid, Pierre, couldn't say 'hello' in French."

The name Charlie Barnet may not ring many bells these days, but Barnet was a famous bandleader in the forties. He came from a wealthy family and operated on a different set of assumptions because of it. When I was booking bands during my first few months at MCA, the big band era was all but over. I told Charlie I could only book a tour for him if he traveled with no more than eight musicians. He agreed, and I started booking a sixteen-week tour that went from Los Angeles up to Vancouver and back down to Salt Lake City—there the tour would end. For these small bands, I'd book mostly nightclubs, not the large ballrooms those guys used to fill. But Charlie started letting local musicians sit in on his sessions and, if he really liked them, he'd hire them for the rest of the tour. By the time the tour hit Fresno, he'd added two men to the band. On his way up the coast, he added four more. His band was now fourteen strong. (In fact, this is how a trumpet player from Eugene, Oregon, got his start. He sat in with Charlie Barnet, and Charlie took him on. The trumpet player's name was Doc Severinsen.)

Naturally, it wasn't long before the headaches started. I had sold this band to small, specialized venues, and when the club operators found out there were eighteen musicians (Charlie wouldn't stop) they called me, furiously demanding, "Where do you expect me to put this big band in my small club?" I could devote two chapters to the Charlie Barnet story, but suffice it to say that Charlie could see no reason why he shouldn't add people to the payroll if he was willing to pay them himself.

Viva Las Vegas

IT WAS 1951, and I was cruising along in the big band department making a fortune for MCA. But there was a problem brewing that I didn't know about. MCA was having a terrible time keeping its booking agents in Las Vegas. They were scared to death of the bosses in those days. They'd be sent to Vegas from the New York or the Chicago offices, but in short order they would be asking MCA to take them off the Vegas accounts—the Reno ones too. Agents new to these towns soon realized the terrifying consequences of slipping up.

In the course of what I think of as my MCA training-for-Vegas tour, I stopped over in Chicago to see Harry Belafonte, the calypso singer from Jamaica who was breaking it up at the Purple Onion. The guy was dynamite. I had been on the Las Vegas job only two weeks when I was asked to book Harry Belafonte into Vegas. Belafonte looked like he had a real future, MCA did not want to lose him, and the one thing Belafonte wanted was to appear in Las Vegas. I tried, and I tried, and I tried, but to no avail. The hotels would not feature "black acts," with the exception of Nat King Cole, Lena Horne, and the Will Mastin Trio, starring Sammy Davis Junior.

I should explain that of the five hotels, MCA booked only four. The Thunderbird was the domain of Hal Braudus. As the house booker, he split the commission on all of the acts he booked, taking five of the standard ten percent. MCA would not split commissions, so I'd never booked an MCA act into the Thunderbird. For Harry Belafonte, however, I went to see Hal Braudus. I raved about the guy. Braudus was so shocked that MCA was selling him an act that he scooped Belafonte up immediately. Elated, I called Belafonte's manager, Jack Rollins (who has since managed such stars as David Letterman, Billy Crystal, Woody Allen, and Robin Williams) and laid out my dilemma. I could get his client into the Thunderbird as an opening act if he agreed to pay an additional five percent to Hal Braudus. But first he had to promise not to let MCA know what I was doing; if anyone found out, it would cost me my job. It helped that by this time Jack and I had formed a mutual admiration society.

To my good fortune, I became a hero on both sides. MCA was pleased that we'd made it into the Thunderbird, and Belafonte couldn't have been happier. On opening night, I felt like Flo Ziegfeld. This isn't to suggest that I wasn't beside myself with anxiety. I thought I'd made a good decision, but I couldn't be sure until I knew that the Thunderbird audience of six hundred thought so too. They did. Harry Belafonte was a smash, and I felt very much a part of it.

Several weeks later, I did the same thing with Rosemary Clooney. Her manager, Joe Shribman, did what Rollins had done and protected me as far as the extra five percent was concerned by paying Hal Braudus directly. I learned something important from the Belafonte booking. During the second week of Harry's engagement, I was driving along the Las Vegas strip. I spotted Belafonte walking, pulled over, and offered him a ride. I was glad to see him again, especially since he was causing such a sensation at the Thunderbird. After I dropped him off in front of the hotel, I saw him walk towards the side entrance. I yelled out of the car window, "Harry, what are you doing? Where are you going?" He said, "Don't you know? Colored folk aren't allowed in the lobby." This came as a shock to me, and it started me wondering: Where did Lena Horne go? Where did Nat King Cole go? I soon found out that they didn't even stay at the hotels they worked in. They stayed in downtown Las Vegas, five miles from the strip.

My next brush with racial issues was of a different sort. The Four Aces had canceled an engagement at the Last Frontier Hotel to do a movie in Rome. Jake Kosloff, the hotel's owner, was really pissed off, and he asked me to book a replacement act, fast. I assured Jake that I'd line up something hot for him—not to worry. My booking sheets told me that a group called the Four Stepbrothers was sensational, although I had never actually seen them perform. At that point, I was traveling back and forth between my L.A. office and Vegas constantly, and on the day the Stepbrothers, I opened flew back to Vegas. On my desk were several messages. All said, in effect, "Jake Kosloff wants to see you right away. Extremely urgent."

I rushed over to the Last Frontier and found the room where the Stepbrothers were rehearsing. Jake was sitting there waiting for me. I looked up at the stage, and I nearly died. The Stepbrothers were a black hoofing act, and I had sold them to Jake as a white singing act to replace the Four Aces. I've been scared only a few times in my life, and this was one of them. I did some fast talking—and some praying.

What saved my career, and perhaps spared me physical injury, was the fact that the Stepbrothers were, indeed, a sensation. The audience went bananas. I went from bum to saint in one day. Theirs was the first standing ovation for an opening act in the history of

Las Vegas. After that, the Stepbrothers worked the strip for many years. Back then, being a black headliner was a hard enough row to hoe; simply making it as a black act was a rare accomplishment. Black performers who could score with an audience were to the Las Vegas entertainment world what Jackie Robinson was to the world of baseball.

Actually, Jake Kosloff was my favorite hotel owner. At that time, I was in my mid-twenties and he was in his mid-sixties. We were quite a pair. He wouldn't buy acts from me unless I got into some gambling action, so he'd be dealing blackjack and I'd be pitching my heart out. In one of our sessions, I lost ninety dollars, a great deal more than I could afford. (My salary from MCA was miniscule, and I was living in a sixty-dollar-a-month room at the Holiday Hotel.) I decided to put the ninety dollars on my expense account as a cost of doing business, which it truly was. MCA didn't see it that way. I told Jake, who called Lew Wasserman and Larry Barnett at MCA and got me off the hook. They paid me the ninety dollars, but they tacked on a "never again" caveat.

I have to say that working in that gambling atmosphere, especially since there were occasions—such as the one I just described—when I had to gamble to do business, was difficult for me. I almost got hooked. Fortunately, I saw what was happening and managed to keep myself under control. It was like giving up drinking, so I can understand what addicted gamblers go through. The whole experience taught me an important lesson about self-control, and I've benefited from it many times over the years.

Early on in my time at MCA, I met Miss Dorothy Foy, who would later become my wife. They brought her in to be my secretary because she knew the routine and could be helpful to me. I soon discovered that Dorothy was one smart lady. She had Phi Beta Kappa keys and rings all over her from the University of California. And she was very perceptive: she could read people and situations in two seconds. She was a pretty, wholesome-looking, very quiet, very reserved, tweed-and-cashmere sort of girl. I had the impression that she was a little schoolmarmish—I know I shocked her a bit when we met. In my inimitable fashion, I said to her, "I'm glad you're working for me. You should know I like my secretary to be a permanent fixture."

"What do you mean by that?" she asked (the perfect straight woman).

"Something I can screw on the desk," I said.

At the time, I thought I was pretty funny. Miss Dorothy Foy did not. She immediately told my boss that she would not work with "that man." But, strangely enough, that was the beginning of a romance that lasted thirty years. We became a twosome, and I gave her the name "Foopie." Why? Well, I made up a song about her, and I'd sing it in the hallway. "Five foot two, eyes of blue, anybody seen Miss Foo, that secretary of mine." There were more words, but these will suffice. Foopie and I had worked and played together for about a year, when one day my boss announced that we could not continue to see each other as long as we were working together at MCA.

Foopie opted to leave. She entered the secretarial pool at Columbia Pictures and, six months later, Harry Cohn asked her to be his private secretary. Owner, president, and CEO of Columbia Pictures, Harry Cohn was the tycoon of the industry, and as his secretary, Foopie had fifty times more power than I did. In 1952, we married. Our marriage got off to a rocky start. First off, Foopie's mother died the week of our wedding, so we postponed the event. Then one night a few weeks later, we were at Ciro's with Mike Meshekoff and Helena Carter. Mike was producer of the number-one television show at the time, *Dragnet*, and Helena was costarring with Cary Grant at Universal. Mike had just bought a Maserati from Jack Warner. After the dinner and show at Ciro's, we were all in high spirits. We decided to pile into Mike's new Maserati and drive to Las Vegas, where Foopie and I could get married.

By 9:00 a.m., I had the license, and I'd booked the chapel of the Flamingo Hotel for our wedding service. Helena was Foopie's bridesmaid, and Mike was my best man; he also gave the bride away. I tried to teach some rock and roll chords to the old geezer on the organ, but after a while I gave up and went to stand next to Foopie. The next thing we knew, we were man and wife.

We headed for our suite at the Flamingo. As Mr. MCA, the man who controlled all the stars, I was given a great suite. They were remodeling the lobby and making everyone take the long way to the elevators, but I knew a shortcut. Grabbing Foopie's hand, I led her through the showroom. I had forgotten that there was a 9:00 a.m. chorus rehearsal. As we charged through, the girls shouted to me, "Hi, honey, how long you in town?"; "Hey, Pierre, where's that dinner you promised me?"; and so on. I hollered back, "I just got married! This is my new wife, Foopie!" We got out of there and found the suite.

Anyway, by now we've been married less than a half an hour. We're in a fabulous hotel suite, the champagne is on ice, a sexy negligee has been sent up from the costume department at my request— and Foopie isn't talking to me. "You didn't tell me you were making out with every chorus girl in Las Vegas!"

It wasn't until eight or nine days later, back home in our apartment, that I finally had sex with my lovely wife. But we were never really a particularly romantic couple. Our private life was intertwined with our work, and we worked late almost every night in those early days. Unlike me, Foopie had little interest in athletics. She tried tennis once, and I tried a hundred times to get her to take golf lessons. I loved everything about show business and, strange as it may seem, given how hard we worked together, she hated everything about the business. For her, it was just a way to make a living. But she had a grand sense of humor, and she always insisted that without humor, you have nothing. She would laugh at all my jokes, but she never told jokes herself. What she had was wit.

We started married life in a tiny one-bedroom apartment in Westwood. Then we made two moves to increasingly better apartments in Hollywood and Beverly Hills before finally buying a house in West Los Angeles, where we lived for twenty-two years.

My early days of booking Las Vegas, Reno, and Lake Tahoe were exciting. These places were as thrilling as the movies suggested they were. Harrah's in Tahoe, Reno, Las Vegas, and Atlantic City is now one huge operation, but it was not always so. When I got started, there was only one Harrah's, and that was in Lake Tahoe. It was a small gambling casino with a showroom that held only sixty-five people. There I would sit in a cubbyhole of an office with Bill Harrah and Candy Hall, his house booker. Since I handled most of the top acts, they would bug me to bag the biggest stars for them. In turn, I would bug them to book some of my lesser stars. This is how I learned about the casino business.

Harrah's could afford to pay Lena Horne or Sinatra fifteen thousand dollars per week to play a room with a capacity of sixty-five because the mere presence of a star of their rank would push the gambling take from, say, ten thousand dollars per night to fifty thousand. Later, Harrah's built a huge new hotel on Lake Tahoe, then another in Reno, another in Las Vegas and, more recently, one in Atlantic City. Whenever I walk into one of these places I remember that small Tahoe hotel, with its tiny office and small casino and restaurant, and those meetings with Bill Harrah and Candy Hall.

The Sahara and the Sands were under construction in Las Vegas during my time there. I took to sitting in the contractor's shacks with Bill Miller at the Sahara and Jack Entratter at the Sands. These gentlemen had been brought to Vegas for obvious reasons: Miller owned Bill Miller's Riviera in New Jersey, and Entratter was the boss of the Copacabana in New York; these were two of the largest and most successful nightclubs in America.

To help launch the new enterprises, the bosses of the five big hotels got together and each volunteered five of their regular stars to the Sands and the Sahara at the maximum price of fifteen thousand dollars a week. The bosses of the five hotels had worked out an ironclad system. Each used leading stars, and each paid those stars fifteen thousand per week, tops. No hotel was permitted to bid on another hotel's acts, and no hotel was permitted to pay an act more than the maximum rate. And remember that in 1953, fifteen thousand dollars a week was huge money.

One day, Flamingo owner Gus Greenbaum, who was by far the toughest of all the Vegas bosses, called me aside and said, "Hey, kid, what's this shit about the Andrews Sisters going to the Sahara and Dennis Day going to the Sands?" I handled both acts, and I assured Gus that there was no way they'd leave the Flamingo. What I didn't know was that Miller and Entratter had been dealing directly with Day and the Andrews Sisters; they were all good buddies from previous New York engagements. Furthermore, word got out that Miller and Entratter had broken the code and were paying the performers twenty-five thousand dollars per week.

In the end, Miller and Entratter changed the course of entertainment history in Las Vegas. Once the fifteen-thousand-dollar ceiling was broken, the going rate climbed. By 1986, for example, Dolly Parton was getting $350,000 per week, and in 1994, Barbra Streisand asked for, and got, one million per show for two nights at the brand new MGM Grand.

I took a lot of bows for starting the entertainment lounge business in Las Vegas, but, like many of life's successes, it came about by accident. I had booked the Mary Kaye Trio into the Last Frontier. Two weeks before the date, the hotel canceled to make room for a major star. The members of the Mary Kaye Trio were not happy, but they agreed to another date. A week before the rescheduled date, the Last Frontier's Jake Kosloff called me to say that Marilyn Maxwell had consented to appear, and he had to cancel the Mary Kaye Trio again. I said, "Jake, you can't do that twice in a row. I'll fly into Vegas and meet you. We have to talk about this."

When I got there, I told Jake that he would have to pay the trio whether they worked or not. He refused.

"You have to—they have a signed contract."

"What can I do?"

"Play them over there."

"Where?"

"By the bar."

"There's no stage."

"We'll build one; we can do it in a day."

"And then what?"

"Then they can do four shows a night."

Up until that time, there was no such thing as a "lounge act" in Las Vegas, not even a lone piano player. The concept was new, and it was scary to everyone—especially to the Mary Kaye Trio, but also to the casino bosses. The bosses didn't want to see audiences leaving the big show and walking right through the casino to catch a smaller show in the lounge. I was extremely nervous. Like I said, the one thing you did not want to do in those days was to cross the casino bosses.

A stage went up in the lounge, the Mary Kaye Trio did their

thing, and the rest is history. After the first week, you couldn't get in to see the Mary Kaye Trio with a hundred-dollar bill. It was such a big hit that a few months later the Sahara started offering lounge acts too—Louis Prima and Keely Smith, followed later by Don Rickles. After that, lounge shows broke out all over Las Vegas. I laugh when I look back on the things I've done to pull myself out of a jam, and coming up with the lounge-act idea was certainly one of them. As Foopie said, "Pierre, that was an act of genius!" We both knew it was a desperate move to save my ass.

It sounds like a line from an old gangster movie: "Kid, if you ever need anything, be sure to call me." But that's what a guy named Doc Stocker used to say to me. I met Doc at the El Rancho, the small, intimate hotel and casino where Howard Hughes lived from 1952 to 1955. I remember booking Tony Bennett into the El Rancho for his first Las Vegas engagement—Tony and I still talk about it. Anyway, Doc was always prodding me with questions: how did I get my job, was I married, and so on. Whenever I'd run into him, he'd say, "Come on, kid, I'll buy you a drink." I learned to love Doc Stocker. I didn't really know what he did at the El Rancho, but I knew he had to be connected in some way. When he walked into any casino in town, everything would come to a stop. Why, I didn't know. Nor did I care.

Then one day, when I was flying back to Vegas from New York, I picked up a magazine that was lying on the seat next to mine. In it was an article about the ten most notorious hoods and racketeers in America. Doc Stocker was among them; there was a photograph of him. I couldn't believe my eyes. I bumped into him a week later in the El Rancho steam room. He was standing in the middle of the room, surrounded by a lot of regulars. Without thinking, I blurted out, "Doc, are you a hood? I read a magazine on the plane, and you were all over it as a hood and a racketeer!"

I've seen rooms clear out fast before, but the guys in this one scattered like buckshot, leaving Doc and me alone together. Doc said, "Look, kid, you can't believe everything you read one hundred percent, but, yes, I've done things in my life I'm not proud of. One day I took a wrong step, and I've been on the same step ever since. Kid, the reason I really like you is because you remind me of when I was a kid. I knew I was going to be a big success, just like you do. I've stayed close to you because I don't want you to get all fucked up like me, with your picture appearing in that magazine one day. I had the opportunity to make it real straight, and I didn't take it. I want you to take the opportunity. Don't get caught up in the good life. It can eat you alive. I'm here to help you over the pitfalls."

The next day, word was all over Las Vegas that I'd called Doc Stocker a hood in the El Rancho steam room. The folklore became that Pierre Cossette was the only man in the world who could talk like that to Doc Stocker.

All of these characters I met during my early days in Las Vegas were guys that the whole country would be reading about a few years later. I used to play golf, for example, with Moe Dalitz, who owned the Desert Inn, and Johnny Rosselli, who was presumably the inn's PR man. Rosselli was always hanging out with the big entertainers of the day. He liked sending private planes to pick them up. Playing golf often with Rosselli, I got to know him. At least, I thought I did. A few years later, he was found dead in a barrel. What I hadn't known was that he had been associated with all the rackets, and some thought he was a go-between for Cuba and the Mob.

Just as I hadn't known who Rosselli really was, I didn't know much about the front guys at the hotels, the ones who held the title of "president." There was Gus Greenbaum at the Flamingo, Wilbur Clark at the Desert Inn, Beldon Kattleman at the El Rancho, Jake

Kosloff at the Last Frontier, and I forget who at the Thunderbird. Although ostensibly these guys were the bosses, anyone with a sharp eye guessed otherwise. You could figure out who the real bosses were when you spotted the "presidents" scrambling into the lobby to meet Mr. So-and-So and his entourage; they'd cater to these visitors all day and wine and dine them into the night.

Sammy Davis Junior was surrounded by these guys and, as we all know, Sammy died with about two percent of the money he should have had. But Sammy had a weakness for gambling and always lived way beyond his means. As a result, he was forever in debt and obligated to "the boys," who would bail him out time and time again. Sammy could, and did, spend two thousand dollars in a day on jewelry for himself and his friends, and it finally did him in financially.

All this changed when Hilton Hotels, Howard Hughes, Del Webb, and other corporate entities started buying or building hotels in Las Vegas. However, the street feeling of Vegas changed too. Now, it's much more like Wall Street than it was in the good old days

The casino bosses who ran things when I was there built Las Vegas after Bugsy Siegel took the initial plunge with his Flamingo Hotel. I was fascinated by the film *Bugsy*, starring Warren Beatty. Those of you who've seen it know that it had to do with the building of the Flamingo, the first hotel on the strip. In the movie's final scene, Bugsy, who is being ousted, is introduced to the man who's taking over: "This is Gus Greenbaum. He's taking over." It gave me a little chill, because Gus was the boss when I took the Vegas job with MCA. Also, the whole story of how the Flamingo was constructed intrigued me. Not only had I spent my early MCA days there and later taken over as entertainment director for the Flamingo Hotel, but also Foopie and I were married there. I could have been the technical director for that movie, but no one asked me.

I had by now become such a hotshot at MCA, controlling a long list of stars, that on opening nights I'd sit ringside with the owner of the hotel and his bigwig guests. I remember the time I booked the Edgar Bergen and Charlie McCarthy show into the Desert Inn. Bergen did a revue type of show; that is, he introduced several acts and then closed with his own. His main feature was his wife, Frances Bergen.

On the night of Edgar's show, I dropped by the performers' dressing rooms, as was my habit, to wish everybody good luck. Frances saw me and grabbed me. "You're just the man I want to see," she said. Feeling pretty important, I asked why. I don't know what I expected her to say, but it certainly wasn't this: the babysitter hadn't shown up, so would I please look after baby Candace? Me, the superstar agent, a babysitter on opening night. But what was I going to say? Through the whole show, I sat in the dressing room, watching Candace Bergen sleep.

The show went extremely well, but the boss was pissed off that I hadn't appeared. When I told him I'd been babysitting, he saw no humor in it at all, even when I told him that it was for the Bergens. But how many people can say that they babysat Murphy Brown backstage while her famous father and mother were performing?

Booking new talent for MCA meant finding performers who hadn't played Las Vegas before. In 1953, someone told me that Mae West was thinking of coming out of retirement. I went gaga over this rumor, and soon I'd arranged a meeting with Mae at her Hollywood penthouse across the street from the Wilshire Country Club. A maid ushered me into a snow-white apartment: the rugs were white, the furniture was white, the cushions were white, the drapes were white, and the lampshades were white. In a few minutes, Mae West walked in, and she, natch, was dressed entirely in white. Man, was she a sight. She was pushing seventy, and she looked all of thirty-two. I was smitten. All I managed to get out of my mouth was,

"Miss West, I'm Pierre Cossette from MCA." She said, "Yes, I know. Have a seat." I sat down, and she announced, "Everything is white here because I'm hot on virginity." These words may not read funny, but just imagine her distinctive voice and her deadpan manner—it was hilarious. For a moment, I just smiled, but one more look from her and I laughed out loud. We then proceeded to talk for hours.

The upshot was that Mae West opened at the Sahara Hotel in Las Vegas in May of that year. In her show, she worked with twelve musclemen recruited from the Mr. Universe Contest. Following Charles Curran's staging and choreography, she would hand a Sahara Hotel room key to each muscleman in turn as she chanted a kind of rap-like verse describing him. She'd coo, "This man here who I introduce to you, won a medal in the weights and the broad jump, too." Each line was funnier than the one before. The Mae West show ended up being an all-time Vegas hit.

One night soon after that success, I was at a Friar's affair in Beverly Hills. Ronald Reagan was the speaker. I was so touched by his story about what happens to an actor when he goes to heaven that the next morning I went to Lew Wasserman and said, "Lew, what about Ronald Reagan for Las Vegas?"

Lew replied, "Are you serious?"

I said, "Absolutely."

Lew shot back, "What in God's name makes you think Ronald Reagan could do a nightclub act?"

"Well," I told him, "I'm putting together an act with five guys. It's being written by Johnny Bradford and Rudolf Friml Junior. I'll offer them a stack of money to book their act in Las Vegas. The only problem is that I'll need only four of them—the lead will have to stay home, because that's the role I want Ronald Reagan to fill. He can do everything the kid does in the act—a little singing, a little dancing, a little comedy. Here's how we'll do it. We'll have some opening talk written for him. Then we'll bring in a film-clip package, and he can narrate his movie career in an unassuming way. We then present the new act with Ronald Reagan playing the lead part. At the end, he finishes with the story he does about what happens to an actor when he goes to heaven. It'll be dynamite. Vegas is dying for new ideas. Ronald Reagan can be the first nonmusical movie star to appear in Vegas!"

Lew was interested enough to bring in Arthur Park and George Chasen of the MCA motion picture department. I could see they were scared to death of the whole idea, but they did agree to set up a meeting between me and Ronald and Nancy Reagan. I went to their home with Johnny Bradford, the writer.

I hit it off immediately with Nancy Reagan (née Davis) because we had some connections. Her father was the longtime partner of Dr. Kanavel, and Davis and Kanavel were the first presidents of the American College of Surgeons. There's a Kanavel-Davis Medical Building at Northwestern University. My sister is married to Dr. Kanavel's son, David. So, as I was relaxing into all of that Kanavel-Davis history, Ronald Reagan asked me what this was all about: "Lew tells me you think I could star in Las Vegas. It's a preposterous idea, but I'm willing to listen, because I'm in a heavy cash crunch right now, and I understand Las Vegas money is tremendous."

I pitched my idea. When I finished, Ronald said, "What about my image? What about the hoods and hookers in the ringside seats? What about the risk to my career if I fail?" It took awhile, but I finally got him to agree to take a good look at the act I had been building. At that time, George Gobel was playing the Hilton in downtown Los Angeles. George was a good friend, and he trusted me. I asked him if I could put the act on for thirty minutes before he went on—as a sort of opening act. George agreed.

A week later, I invited Ronald and Nancy Reagan to the Hilton to see the act. "Remember," I said, "keep your eye on the guy in the middle; that's your part." After the show, Ronald said, "You know,

I can do everything he does. Maybe you've got something here. See how much you can get in Las Vegas and let me consider the offer." As for Nancy, she loved the idea and urged her husband to do it. Lew Wasserman couldn't believe that Ronald Reagan was interested. I went to Jake Kosloff at the Last Frontier and got from him a firm offer of fifteen thousand dollars a week for four weeks. Reagan liked the offer, and the show was on.

I must tell you that the man got cold feet several times before opening night. The day before, he wanted to cancel. I believe that it was his training as an actor and the fact that he was a trouper that got him through, but this isn't to say that I didn't have a hand in holding it all together. In the end, Ronald Reagan was an enormous hit. Yet, even though the act brought him all kinds of offers, he never did it again.

Thirty years later, I took my son John to the Frank Sinatra opening at the Universal Amphitheater in Hollywood. John was a major Reagan fan. The fact that we were sitting in Frank's section next to the rich and famous of Hollywood meant little to him, but Ronald Reagan was his hero. Ten minutes before show time, a hush came over the crowd of six thousand. Everybody stood, and there was resounding applause as Ronald and Nancy Reagan came down the stairs and started making their way to their seats in Frank Sinatra's private section. They spotted me and headed over. Johnny was dumbstruck. Ronald and Nancy put out their hands and said, "Hi, Pierre." Ronald kidded, "How much do you think we could get in Vegas now?" Before I could answer, Nancy quipped, "More than Dolly Parton?"

Today if you asked John, who has by now seen it all, to name his biggest showbiz thrill, I know that he'd say it was that night with Ronald Reagan.

Red Skelton needed an opening act for his Las Vegas debut at the Sahara Hotel that year. I'd seen sixteen-year-old Anna Maria Alberghetti sing at a party, and I thought she was sensational. The girl was a child prodigy who had no stage experience outside of classical concerts, but I talked Red and his wife, Georgia, into taking her.

It wasn't easy. And the next step was no easier: I had to talk Papa Alberghetti, who spoke no English, into letting his daughter perform in what he considered a city of sin. His Italian friends assured him that Vegas was no place for his young daughter. But Papa Alberghetti wanted to move the family back to Italy, and they were broke. The money I offered was too much for him to turn down.

My next move was to put an act together for Anna Maria. I knew of a young composer who was under contract to Universal as an arranger. I thought he was a big talent, and I approached him to do Anna Maria's act. His name was Henry Mancini. Henry was excited about putting together his first nightclub act—and he became even more excited when he heard Anna Maria sing at the first rehearsal.

On opening night, the place was jammed; Red Skelton was a superstar, and this was his first Las Vegas appearance. To say Anna Maria was a hit would be a gross understatement. In her sixteen-minute performance she totally wowed them.

Prior to her debut with Red Skelton, I had booked her for one night at the Shrine Auditorium as one of the acts for the annual firemen's ball. My intention was to give her a chance to break in her new act. Anna Maria spoke English with a very strong, but cute, Italian accent. I wrote something for her to say at her final bow. This is what the fine young Italian lady said in her charming broken English: "There is nothing in the world I like better than firemen's balls." (Politicians do not have exclusive rights to dirty tricks.) This brand of humor might not make it today, but that night what started as a titter around the room soon became an uproar of sidesplitting laughter. A few of Papa Alberghetti's Italian-speaking friends explained the play on words to him, and soon he was looking for me. Before he could find me, I disappeared into the night.

Well, a week after Anna Maria's success at the Sahara with Red Skelton, a man who had seen her perform that night called me to make a deal. He gave his name as Howard Hughes. Apparently, he had checked with several people, who told him I was the key to any deal with Anna Maria Alberghetti. I told Lew Wasserman and Herman Citron at MCA about the call. What did they want me to do? They both declared, "Follow up on it. It's your department." I was only two years out of college, and here I was talking with Howard Hughes, one of the world's most famous people.

After Hughes and I had exchanged a few more calls, we arranged to meet in a Westwood restaurant at 6:00 p.m. I showed up; he didn't. Through Foopie, I had gotten to know Harry Cohn of Columbia Pictures quite well. His advice was to stay away from Howard Hughes. "He is a bad man, and a kid like you has no business going up against him." In the course of the next two months, I had several more calls from Howard. (Yes, I called him Howard, not Mr. Hughes.) Once he called me at home and asked if I was alone. I said, "No, my wife is with me." He said, "Tell her to leave." I did. Foopie walked out the back door, but in a few seconds she came rushing back in, shouting, "How dare he say I have to leave my own home! Tell that idiot what Harry Cohn had to say about him!" I quickly covered the phone with my hand, hoping Hughes hadn't heard her. I guess he hadn't, because this routine went on for another two weeks—two more calls, two more scheduled meetings. He never showed up.

Sometime later, when I was back in Las Vegas, I got a call from a Howard Hughes representative. He apologized for the missed

meetings, but "Mr. Hughes's presence was in such demand"—
"Things came up at the last minute," and so on. Now Hughes wanted
to meet me at 1:00 a.m. in the Sahara Hotel coffee shop. The representative promised me that Hughes would be there, and I had to
promise him that I would be alone. I arrived promptly at 1:00. By
2:30, there was still no Howard Hughes. Knowing that there was a
flight that left Las Vegas at 3:00 a.m. for Los Angeles, I grabbed a
cab and headed for the airport. As we were landing at Los Angeles
International Airport, at 4:15 a.m., those passengers who were looking out the windows started to buzz. Two police cars were following
us to the gate, their lights flashing. When the ramp was lowered,
three policemen stepped on board before anyone could leave. One
of them asked the flight attendant, "Do you have a passenger named
Cossette on board?"

I was stunned. I felt like public enemy number one, finally captured. They put me in one of the cruisers and whisked me away to
a waiting TWA Constellation. I finally managed to ask, "What is
this all about?" The cops said, "Mr. Hughes is sorry he missed the
meeting, but he'll see you in the same coffee shop at 6:00 a.m."

Do I have to tell you? He didn't show up. This Hughes thing
was turning into a saga. Again, he called to apologize. Our next
date was for dinner at the Sahara Hotel, a week later, at 7:00 p.m. He
assured me that he would definitely be there. Lo and behold, when
I walked into the hotel restaurant, there he was. At first, I couldn't
believe it was Howard Hughes. He looked more like one of the home-
less we see these days in big cities. I don't know if my face registered
it or not, but I was shocked that the famous Howard Hughes looked
like something the cat dragged in.

I knew that he had once attempted to turn pro in golf, so I
started to make small talk on that subject. My natural jovial manner
usually wins people over, but this guy was having none of it. He got

right down to business. He wanted to know everything about Anna Maria. "Look," he started in, "I think this Anna Maria Alberghetti girl is terrific. I want to make her a superstar. I did it for Jane Russell, and I can do it for her. I want to put her under contract for records, personal appearances, motion pictures, television, and concerts—the whole ball of wax. I will pay her handsomely for an exclusive arrangement. I understand you are the key to making the deal. I have one condition: you are not to tell anyone at MCA what our deal is. I know that makes it tough for you, but I want to do it all with a side letter to you and her father."

I couldn't believe what I was hearing, but there it was. However, there was no way I wasn't going to report this to Lew Wasserman.

"What about her schooling?" he persisted. "She's only sixteen. We have to consider that."

"She's been going to school on the Paramount lot," I said. "She did a movie there with Bing Crosby."

Hughes glared at me and said, "This girl has done a motion picture?"

"Yes."

"Why didn't you tell me this?" He was turning mean and angry.

"You never asked me. You never showed up until tonight."

Hughes was livid. He walked out without even saying goodbye. In fact, he left before his steak arrived. I stayed and ate mine, hoping he had at least picked up the tab. Of course, he hadn't. Afterwards I told Foopie, "You were right. That man is very strange. Harry Cohn will love knowing that I got stuck with the check after all those months of negotiation." I became very respectful of Foopie's take on people after that.

Foopie had been working for Cohn for a year. At that point, I was producing a show involving the whole Alberghetti family—Mama, Papa, Anna Maria, sister Carla, and brother Paulo—complete with a symphony orchestra and "dancing waters," water sprinklers that we used to create dramatic theatrical effects on stage. I booked the act into the Royal Nevada Hotel, now known as the Aladdin. The concept of using a classical orchestra, classical music, and "dancing waters" was a brand new one for Las Vegas, and the show was the first major production for Foopie's husband.

Cohn sent telegrams inviting every superstar in Hollywood to attend the opening night of Pierre Cossette's show at the Royal Nevada. No one knew who Pierre Cossette was, but they came, and they came in droves. I've never seen so many stars assembled in one place in my life, before or since. Among the guests were Cary Grant, Humphrey Bogart, Kim Novak, and Rita Hayworth. And, sitting together at a big table at the opening night dinner party were Foopie and Harry Cohn.

The show was a smash. When the curtain fell, I was backstage. I heard the audience cheering and shouting "Encore!" and I broke up. That show made my career as a theatrical producer: I had put it together from top to bottom, and I was very proud of my accomplishment. But Harry Cohn hadn't gone to those lengths just to promote Anna Maria Alberghetti; his main motivation was to do something nice for his secretary and her young producer-husband. Throughout the show, Foopie couldn't stop crying on her boss's shoulder; she was so excited for me. That was my first venture away from MCA, and, thanks to Foopie, it got me off to a slam-bang start. The press covered the opening and put me into the front line. Now I was a producer. Not an agent: a producer.

One day, the owner of the Flamingo Hotel said to me, "Hey, kid, I need somebody like Bill Miller or Jack Entratter, somebody who has a personal relationship with these stars. You represent most of them.

What does a kid like you make? Five hundred a week? I'll give you eight hundred bucks a week to work for me. You'll be the entertainment director of the Flamingo Hotel."

I stalled him so I could talk it over with Charlie Mapes. Charlie was a buttoned-down Brooks Brothers type who wore tweed sports coats with leather elbow patches. He was a Harvard graduate to boot—all in all, a far cry from your typical casino guy. At the death of his father, he had become the owner of the Mapes Hotel. I knew if I talked to him, he'd give me an objective answer. When I saw him, later in the week, I said, "Charlie, I got an offer last week from the Flamingo in Las Vegas to become their entertainment director."

"Are you going to take it?"

"I wanted to talk to you about it first."

"What do you want to know?"

"Well, I'm a little concerned that if I take a job like that, I'll end up wearing alligator shoes, white suits, and a tie with a diamond in it—and I'll have a hooker on my arm."

"That won't happen. Look at me, I've been around it all my life. Just be who you are, and the wise guys will respect you and leave you alone. By the way, that's a hell of an idea. You could be my entertainment director too. Instead of booking an act for two weeks in Nevada, you could do four—two at the Flamingo and two at the Mapes. It would save me money, because the acts would love doing Vegas and Reno back-to-back. By the way, how much did they offer?"

I said, "Eight hundred per week."

Charlie said, "Look, I'm not giving you eight hundred a week, but I'll give you four hundred."

A couple of days later, I talked it over with Foopie. We were still living in an eighty-five-dollar-a-month apartment on Veteran Avenue in Westwood. I was making almost two hundred per week, including my Christmas bonus, and Foopie was making $150 working for Harry Cohn. All of a sudden, I was looking at the prospect of making twelve hundred dollars a week on my own. The question was, should I leave MCA? Foopie thought so. She said, "You aren't good at in-fighting, Pierre. You aren't cutthroat enough—you can't even fire people. As much as I love you, and as bright as I know you are, you're not cut out for the corporate life."

It was an agonizing decision, but together we decided to go for it. The day before I was to leave, Lew Wasserman called and asked me to come to his office. He was at his desk when I got there, and I sat down in a chair facing him. Lew picked up a Steuben glass paperweight and said, "Pierre, what do you think would happen if I threw this out the window?" I had no idea where he was going with this, so I simply said, "I don't know."

"It would hit some young man who had got so caught up with the stars, the limos, the ringside tables, and all the glamour that goes with being associated with MCA that he decided to quit and go out on his own," Lew said. "The reason it's bound to hit someone like that is because they're all walking around the building trying to get back in." A million thoughts flew in and out of my head in the one minute before I answered him. I said, "Lew, I've got to do this. I've got to make it on my own."

I left that meeting with many misgivings, which lasted for more than a year, but I was walking into an income that was six times higher than the one I'd been pulling in at MCA. And I had a strong support system in Foopie. So, overnight, while I was still in my twenties, I became the largest buyer of live talent in the United States. Instead of trying to sell all the top acts, I was now trying to buy all the top acts. I loved the challenge of coming up with new concepts. Although concepts can lead to high-risk ventures, they are the stuff of showbiz. If you have a good concept, it's as good as having a top star, and it can cost much less: when you come up with a new idea that works, you can repeat it every year.

When I left MCA, Marty Melcher asked me to share space with him on the Sunset Strip, and I quickly agreed. It was exciting for me, because Marty was married to Doris Day, who was then the number-one box office star and top-selling recording artist. Marty, who didn't like the idea of being known as Doris Day's husband, concentrated heavily on the music side of the business, although he did deal with the movie side too. We shared the rent on a two-office suite, and we each had a secretary.

Marty's side of the office was Daywin Productions, for movies, and Arwin Productions, for recording and music publishing. My side was simply "Pierre Cossette." My accounts were the Flamingo Hotel in Las Vegas and the Mapes Hotel in Reno. I was also personal manager for singing stars Anna Maria Alberghetti, Vic Damone, and Jane Morgan, as well as Metropolitan Opera star Helen Traubel and Broadway star John Raitt. It was a pretty good start in the business for a young guy, but I was still apprehensive. Could I really do it on my own? I believed I could, and Foopie certainly backed me up, and that's what seemed to matter in the end. The association with Marty was good for me. He had previously been married to Patty Andrews of the Andrews Sisters, and he knew his stuff. I learned a lot about recording and music publishing from Marty, and that became important a few years later, when I started my own music-publishing company.

Yet I was still in many ways a star-struck kid, and I found myself spending a lot of time on movie sets with Doris Day. Even though I met directors and movie producers and learned a few things about the process of making films, before long I saw that I was letting myself get sidetracked. It was time for me to part company with Marty and put my nose to the grindstone. At this point,

Foopie was a still a bigger figure in show business than I was. Marty, and many top agents (including some from MCA), would call her, or ask me to call her, to request an appointment with Harry Cohn.

When the Flamingo's convention manager approached me and said, "We've got a major medical convention coming in May; these people have money to spend, and we need a big star to get 'em into the Flamingo," I staged one of my most unique acts for that venue.

Try as I might, I could not get a big star. Finally, I had an idea. All hotels had huge chorus lines in those days. They were a big attraction, especially since most people who went to Vegas to gamble were men. I placed ads in the help-wanted sections of the major newspapers in New York, Miami, Chicago, Seattle, San Francisco, Dallas, Milwaukee, Detroit, Denver, and a few other cities. The ad said: "The Flamingo Hotel in Las Vegas wants to build a chorus line of doctors. Please send eight-by-ten photo, plus proof of your doctorate."

Somewhere in my files, I have the hundreds of responses I received. I couldn't believe that there were so many women with doctorates who were willing, even eager, to be part of a chorus line. I needed only sixteen of them. Poring over the photos, I selected about twenty-two possibilities; that is, women who were either attractive or cute, with nice figures and the right look. Most of them, I later discovered, had harbored a secret desire to become a singer or a dancer, and they saw this unlikely offer as a chance to make their dreams come true.

Once I felt confident that I could pull it off, I went back to the Flamingo boss and said, "Okay, I've got an act for your medical convention. It's called 'the Dancing Doctors.'" I could tell he thought I was crazy. It would take another book to describe how I actually put an amateur chorus line together with these lady doctors from all parts of America. But I did. I made sure that their academic credentials were listed in the program next to their names. The final mix was eighty percent medical doctors and twenty percent PhDs in various disciplines: engineering, education—you name it. When they turned out to be a major hit, the women themselves were as thrilled as anybody.

No one had told the casino boss that the Dancing Doctors wasn't a real Vegas act. On the third night, he came over to me and said, "What's the matter with these broads? They don't mix with the customers. They should be in the casino and in the lounge between shows and after the shows. They don't have to have sex with the customers—I'm not saying that—but, goddammit, they either mix or they're out the door."

I couldn't wait to call the girls together to explain the rules of the game. As I suspected, they found it all as hilarious as I did. More than half of them had brought their husbands with them. They decided as a group that they would go along with it and do some "mixing." Keeping a straight face, I went to the casino boss and informed him that I had arranged for him to meet with the girls one hour before show time to explain his position. This is what he said to them: "I called you broads together to explain our system here. Now we don't expect you to give no head, and we're not asking you to climb in bed with the customers. We're just asking you to mix. If a high roller wants you to have a drink with him, have a drink with him. I'll tell you who the high rollers are."

And so the "broads" ended up having the time of their lives. At the end of the two weeks, they told me that it had been the most exciting thing that had ever happened to them. They were reluctant to go back to their normal lives.

Pulling off my next concept for the Flamingo, I didn't have such smooth sailing. By this time, *Amos 'n' Andy*, already solid as a radio show, was making it on television. On the strength of the show's reputation, I was able to talk the hotel owner into letting me put an act together for Amos and Andy. It was a tough call, because Las Vegas had never before featured an all-black show.

I went to see if Amos and Andy themselves would be interested. Both of them had come up through vaudeville, so they knew all about nightclub engagements, and, yes, they were very interested. Next, I put together a one-and-a-half-hour show. We rehearsed it, and then I arranged an engagement at D'Amato's Supper Club in Portland, Oregon, to break it in. The show was a hit. When it closed, we flew back to Los Angeles, where we'd spend the week remaining before the Flamingo opening. All of Las Vegas was a-flutter. Everyone knew that as successful as Amos and Andy were, this would be the first all-black show to play Vegas, and it could either bomb or be a big hit. The Flamingo boss was reassured because the Portland date had gone so well, and he was becoming excited about the opening. But his excitement was short-lived.

The day before the opening, the real-life Andy shot the real-life Amos for stealing a roast beef out of the refrigerator. To make matters worse, he shot him in the ass. As you can imagine, this made huge headlines across the country. With Andy in jail and Amos in the hospital, we had to cope with bad publicity and—it seemed—a delayed opening. But, to our immense relief, Andy was released because Amos would not press charges. Amos recovered and the show opened, only ten days late, to a media blitz. It was standing room only. Who knows whether the show would have been such a hit without the unplanned notoriety that came our way? Sometimes, you just plain luck out.

Whether it was for the Mapes Hotel in Reno or the Flamingo Hotel in Las Vegas, the biggest part of my job was seeking out new talent, new stories, new ideas. I was at it constantly. One day, I happened to be reading *Life* magazine, and on the cover was a picture of Paul Anderson. Anderson had won Olympic gold for weightlifting, and he was everyone's current favorite all-American boy. A lightbulb flashed in my head. I called Charlie Mapes and asked him what a silver dollar weighed. He asked me why I wanted to know, but I wouldn't tell him. Even so, he called the next day with the answer.

My idea was to have Paul Anderson demonstrate to an audience how many silver dollars he could lift. I figured that the coins could be stacked in two Lucite boxes joined by a crossbar. Anderson would lift the coin-filled barbell and then invite audience members to come to the stage and give it a try. Those who succeeded—but of course no one could—would be allowed to keep the money.

I assured Charlie Mapes that Anderson was the only man on Earth capable of lifting this weight; he'd proven it at the Olympics. Charlie thought it was a terrific idea, but he insisted that Lloyds of London insure the barbell. After all, he said, the Mapes Hotel presented two shows per night, and together the two boxes would contain close to forty thousand silver dollars. Unfortunately, Lloyds would not insure the thing, and Charlie ordered me to cancel the show. I tried to tell him what Paul Anderson had told me—that even though there were bigger and stronger men than he, they'd never be able to lift this weight. It all had to do, he'd explained, with leverage and the laws of physics. But Charlie would not budge. "Cancel," he said. So I quickly responded, "Charlie, I think I can get this on *The Ed Sullivan Show*."

In the fifties, *The Ed Sullivan Show* was all the rage. Getting a remote telecast on the show was nearly impossible, but I knew Ed Sullivan and his producer, Bob Precht, and I had a strong hunch that this Americana concept would appeal to them. The prospect excited even Charlie Mapes. So off I went to New York to meet with Sullivan and Precht, and, go figure, I came out with a commitment! *The Ed Sullivan Show* would pick up Paul Anderson live from the Mapes Hotel in Reno. "Charlie, this is worth millions to you," I said, and he agreed. I was riding high.

On the morning of Thursday, June 28, I was on a plane to Reno with Paul Anderson, who was busy consuming boxes of strength-building gelatin. The barbell had been sent on ahead. Paul did not plan to rehearse, because, as he said, it would involve lifting too much weight in one day. The plane circled the Reno airport before landing, and I was thrilled to see nearly a hundred private planes parked below. This was a sure sign that Piper, Lear, or Gulfstream was having a private airplane manufacturers' convention, and there would be plenty of conventioneers in town.

The Mapes Hotel lobby looked like a locker-room—it was filled with huge muscular guys. I couldn't figure it out. Then the bell captain handed me a fistful of messages from Charlie Mapes, all saying, "See me the minute you arrive. Extremely urgent!" Charlie Mapes was fuming. Why? Because Reno was not hosting an airplane manufacturers' convention. The private airplanes I had seen at the airport had transported a hundred huge lumberjack gorillas to town, each of them ready to make a killing at the Mapes Hotel's weightlifting show.

On opening night, Charlie sat next to me, ringside, holding my arm in a death grip, just in case something went wrong and I tried to take flight. But what could go wrong? So what if Paul Anderson was five-foot-seven and the guys in the audience ranged up to six-foot-nine and averaged 275 pounds?

The moment arrived. The lights went down. The band began to play. Band leader Eddie Fitzpatrick announced, "Ladies and gentlemen, welcome to the Mapes Hotel. We have a great show for you tonight: Bud and Cece Robinson, comedian Dave Barry, and the star of our show, Olympic gold medallist Paul Anderson, making his nightclub debut." The curtain opened, Bud and Cece were terrific, and Dave Barry was hilarious. Then out came the star of our show. We had choreographed and rehearsed it all. Following the music, Paul circled the weight setup, moving back and forth, to and fro. Then he crouched down, positioned his shoulders under the bar, and prepared to lift the forty thousand silver dollars. I couldn't believe what I was seeing . . . my God! The floor was caving in! Paul Anderson, still holding the barbell, was standing on tiptoes. The veins in his neck and along his arms were bulging, and his face was a red-purple color.

As luck would have it, the floor held, and Anderson completed the act, but I had a vision—both comic and tragic—of Anderson and the forty thousand coins dropping sixteen flights from the Skyroom to the hotel lobby. The look on Charlie Mapes's face told me that he, too, was caught between panic and relief: panic at what had nearly happened, and relief that the whole grueling episode was over and he wouldn't be facing any lawsuits. What he hadn't anticipated, however, was the reaction of the one hundred gorillas and their sponsors. To shouts of "Fraud!" "Setup!" "We've been had!" Charlie and I slipped out the back exit.

"Thank God that's over! We have to cancel the show," Charlie said. "What about *The Ed Sullivan Show* on Sunday?" I said. "We can't cancel on Ed Sullivan." We argued that point for hours, until I finally got his okay. In came the cranes and other heavy equipment to reinforce the Skyroom stage. Meanwhile, on Friday, on Saturday, and for most of Sunday, the gorillas and the handlers continued to fume, convinced that the whole thing was a hoax. To make matters worse, most of them were losing heavily at the gambling tables. Not a happy bunch, but they remained under control because they anticipated that their big chance would come on Sunday night, during *The Ed Sullivan Show.*

Two minutes before airtime, I was backstage speaking to Ed in New York on a walkie-talkie. Everything was in place. The countdown started, and suddenly I saw Charlie Mapes hanging a sandwich board over Paul Anderson that read "Mapes Hotel, Reno." Ed Sullivan saw it too, and he screamed through the speaker, using language you wouldn't believe. "Take that sign off, and take it off *now*!" yelled Ed. Charlie shouted to Paul, "Keep it on! It's my hotel!"

Paul Anderson was obviously terrified. He did nothing. Fifteen seconds before he took the stage, I reached over and pulled the sign off him. Paul was a hit, and Ed Sullivan was pleased as punch. The city of Reno was ecstatic. Paul stayed on for two weeks, doing two shows per night. And the gorillas? They hung around for a week, and one by one they gave it a try at each of the two nightly (jam-packed) shows. A couple came close, but no one but Paul was able to lift the weight.

Every year, Charlie Mapes put on his annual Duck Feed. He'd invite all of his high-roller customers from Oregon, Utah, Idaho, California, and beyond, and he'd feed them duck prepared by a chef imported from New Orleans. As entertainment director of the Mapes Hotel, it was my job to get a star performer to appear at the Duck Feed. After several years, I had run out of friends to do the show. It didn't help that they had to work for free. Charlie thought that providing them with a duck dinner, hotel accommodation, and airfare was payment enough. Andy Williams, Vic Damone, Jim Backus, and Rowan and Martin had all done the show for me in previous years.

I finally convinced Charlie that his best bet was to bring in an unknown. At the time, Don Rickles fit that description. He was working at the tiny but hip Slate Brothers Club on La Cienega in Beverly Hills. I knew Don from Miami. I told him to consider this as a favor to me and added that he'd also boost his career by appearing before all those Nevada movers and shakers.

Because Don was an insult comedian, I had to establish certain ground rules for this event: 1. Do not knock the food (Charlie Mapes was extremely proud of his cuisine); 2. Don't mention speedboats (Charlie had cracked up every speedboat he'd ever owned, and he deeply resented any reference to it); 3. Do not mention Charlie's mother (Charlie was a mommy's boy, and everyone in Reno knew it).

At show time, I was sitting with Charlie, who was very dubious about presenting a newcomer. He glared at me with his "This better be good!" look. The announcer said, "Gentlemen, Charles Mapes is proud to present a new comedian! Don Rickles," and Rickles launched in: "Good evening, gentlemen. How about the food tonight? They wouldn't feed this slop to prisoners. And did you hear that speedboat crash in the lobby and see the old broad jump in and breast-feed Charlie?" The audience was in an uproar.

After the show, I had to keep Charlie and Don apart. I was afraid that Charlie would kill Don, but when people started complimenting Charlie on the show, he finally calmed down. As for me, I came out of it just fine. The owner of the Riverside Hotel in Reno came up to me after the show and said, "Hey, that guy's terrific. I have Fran Warren opening in a couple of weeks and I need a comic. Is he available?"

"How much can you pay him?"

"How much would he want?

"A thousand a week."

"Okay."

Don was making three hundred dollars a week at the Slate Brothers Club, and to him that was the big time. Together, we called his agent, Joe Rollo, to see if Rollo could clear two weeks from the Slate brothers, and he did. Mapes's Duck Feed was the first time Don Rickles played the state of Nevada. Within a few years, that thousand a week in Reno had become two hundred thousand a week in Vegas, Reno, and Tahoe.

In Las Vegas, the Sands Hotel was turning into a hotbed of stars and theatrical activity. The fifteen-thousand-dollar-per-act arrangement among the big hotels was now a thing of the past, and Bill Miller of the Sahara and Jack Entratter of the Sands were the chief raiders. There was hardly a nightclub star of any stature who hadn't worked for them.

One of the less ostentatious signs that the Sands Hotel was now on top was the fact that its steam room had become the meeting place of the stars. Between 5:00 and 7:00 p.m., before show time, every star playing Vegas headed over to the Sands for a steam and a massage. It was all very exclusive: only those who obtained Entratter's approval could use the facilities between those hours, and each was issued his own Sands bathrobe, not a standard blue one—the mark of the outsider. Even people like Dean Martin had to check with Jack first if he wanted to bring in a guest. The white terry bathrobes had the star's names on the front and nicknames on the back. Dean Martin was "Dino Baby," Joe E. Lewis was "Champ," Don Rickles was "Venom." This in-group also included the likes of Bing Crosby, Nat King Cole, Bob Newhart, Jerry Lewis, Joe DiMaggio, and Frank Sinatra. As the MCA guy who had all the stars in his hip pocket, I was a frequent visitor to the steam room as a guest of one of my clients or of Jack himself.

One day, Jack called me in my room at the Flamingo and said, "Hey, Frenchman, come on down to the Sands and join me for a steam. Be there at 5:30." At 5:30, I walked into the steam room, passing one superstar after another. I found Jack, and he took me over to the rack where the stars hung their robes. He ceremoniously handed me one. The front read "Pierre Cossette," and the back read "The Frenchman." It still stands out as one of the biggest thrills of my many years in showbiz.

Back in the fifties, the personal managers—the people who mainly managed lounge acts and opening acts—formed the Conference of Personal Managers. At that time, I think Joe Rollo had the biggest star: Billy Eckstine. I had just started managing Anna Maria Alberghetti. Red Doff, the president of the Conference of Personal Managers, came up with a great idea. "We should do something for our community," he said. "A benefit for a hospital, or something like that. We'll put all our acts together and put on a hell of a show."

We all agreed. With the help of a publicist friend, we were able to entice Mrs. Norman Chandler, owner of the *Los Angeles Times*, to provide us with a good concept for a charity event. She and some of her friends asked to meet with us. We wanted to give them special treatment, so we arranged a lunch at the exclusive Beverly Hills Club. The party consisted of twenty-six personal managers and nineteen elegant ladies. The ladies arrived in chauffeur-driven limousines. It had the look of a prestigious society gig, at least from where we were sitting. If the ladies were expecting to find Darryl Zanuck, Cecil B. DeMille, Harry Cohn, Dore Schary, Lew Wasserman, and other show business leaders, they were probably surprised to see us—a bunch of ragamuffins, some of whom hadn't worn a tie for years, if ever.

It was an awkward situation, and I must say I was quite uneasy. The ladies seemed to be thinking, "How did we get into this?" And Mrs. Chandler looked perplexed. The ladies were all seated across a long table from the managers. Then Red Doff got up and said, "Ladies and gentlemen, we all know why we're here." Turning to the managers, he continued: "Now I think we should tell the ladies what it is we plan to do for them."

I was sitting next to Maurice Duke, who said, "Hey, Red, why should we tell the broads what we're doin' for them? Let the broads tell us what they're gonna do for us." It was right out of *Guys and Dolls*. Everybody stared. I couldn't hold it in any longer. I started to laugh, it grew into a belly laugh, and soon everyone was laughing loudly—including the ladies.

When people ask, "Is show business different today?" I say, "Yes, very." There's no room for the street guys anymore. College boys have replaced the old-style players. In fact, I was among the first of the college boys. If I had not been a USC graduate when I entered the business, I probably wouldn't have made it.

In the late fifties, which I call my "personal management years," I represented Vic Damone, who was then a huge motion picture and singing star. Around that time, I had seen Herb Jeffries close his act at the Royal Nevada Lounge by walking through the audience singing his biggest hit, "Flamingo." When he reached the slot machines at the side of the room he'd drop in a coin, pull the handle, and end his song on that beat. He had no microphone in his hand, and I couldn't figure out how he did it. But I loved it.

I called his manager and asked him to explain it to me, and he told me about the tiny new sound device called a "lavaliere" microphone, which the performer could attach to his clothing. Jeffries had it on his jacket lapel. These days, if you look closely, you can usually spot it on talk-show hosts and their guests, but back then it was quite a novelty.

A week later, Vic Damone was opening at the Flamingo Hotel in Las Vegas. I told him how fabulous his act would be if he did it with this virtually invisible microphone. For one thing, it would drive the women crazy to see him stroll casually around the stage with his hands free. He wasn't comfortable with the idea, but he agreed to try it.

Twenty minutes before show time, Vic called me to his dressing room and said, "I'll do it for the second show, but not the opening." When I asked him why, he answered, "I just found out that all the MGM guys plus all the network bigwigs are in the audience, and I just don't want to chance it." For the next twenty minutes, I talked to him, insisting that this new look would excite the bigwigs and that he'd blow it if he waited until the second show. Reluctantly, he agreed. I was one hundred percent right. Vic strolled across that stage, his voice perfectly amplified, with no microphone showing. The audience loved it. I was sitting back musing that Frank Sinatra, Tony Bennett, Johnny Mathis, and others would soon pick up on it.

Halfway through his act, Vic was doing a slow-ballad version of "Come Rain or Come Shine" when out of nowhere a police call came over the sound system. "Car 26, armed robbery in progress, 1392 26th Street. Backups in the area deploy immediately." Clearly shaken, Vic kept going: "I'm going to love you like nobody's loved you, come rain or come shine." Then: "Car 42, fight outside Golden Nugget."

I was afraid my career was over. Vic had a temper, and when his audience started to giggle, then laugh, then applaud loudly, I wasn't sure what he was going through. I could see that the audience was taking it as a clever, well-executed bit. Vic managed to change micro-phones and finish his show. Later—after Vic had forgiven me—I received calls from people wanting to know the name of the writer who had come up with that great police-call routine.

Just to give you an idea of the kinds of crazy mishaps that befall the stars, when Anna Maria Alberghetti was playing in *Carnival* on Broadway, she exited the stage on cue and had two minutes before she was to go on again. Naturally, she went to the bathroom, peed, and flushed the toilet—but she had forgotten to turn off her button microphone. It didn't take the audience or the actors on stage long to figure out what they were hearing. The whole night was hilarious. I remember it well. Anna Maria went on to win the Tony Award for Best Actress in a Musical.

One of my favorite Anna Maria Alberghetti stories has to do with her getting a star on Hollywood Boulevard. Papa Alberghetti understood publicist Warren Cowan to say that Anna Maria had been given a star on a Hollywood walk of fame, but for some reason he couldn't get Warren to tell him exactly where. All Warren would say, apparently, was "Don't worry." Papa, totally frustrated, decided to find out for himself. He took over the backroom of Patsy D'Amora's restaurant in Hollywood and invited every Italian he knew to join him. Real Italians. Very few of whom could speak English. All in all, there were twenty-two Italians—and me.

Papa took out a huge map of Hollywood and spread it on a table. He then assigned each of us a six-block area to search for Anna Maria's star. We had two hours before we had to report back. One by one, we returned to the restaurant, mission unaccomplished. You can imagine what happened when the last straggler came in with the same news: Anna Maria's star was nowhere to be found. Papa flew into a rage. But, after blowing his top in the true Italian spirit, he turned his attention to the dinner—a feast of pasta, bread, and wine. There was much boisterous talk and conviviality.

Was Warren Cowan premature in mentioning Anna Maria's star to Papa? Yes. What he actually meant to say was that she *would* get a star, on Hollywood Boulevard. Did Anna Maria ever get her star? Yes, four years later.

Then there's the story about Mama Alberghetti. When Anna Maria was white-hot in the business, Edward R. Murrow had a show called *Person to Person*. He'd take a camera crew into a celebrity's home, and the celebrity would show them around, cooing things like, "This is our living room; this is our dining room; this is our dog," and so forth. Murrow wanted Anna Maria, and I thought it would be terrific exposure for her. Also, since she was the only fluent English speaker in the family, she'd have to be the main attraction. The only big diversion would be in the kitchen, where Mama Alberghetti, who was a great cook, would greet everybody. The camera would follow Anna Maria into the kitchen just as Mama was getting ready to take her lasagna out of the oven.

Well, it seems that Papa had a friend who was the chef at the prestigious LaRue's restaurant in Hollywood. LaRue's was even more expensive than Chasen's. A lot of stars hung out there. Papa told his chef friend that the family was going to be featured on *Person to Person*, and that when the camera crew reached the kitchen they were going to zoom in on a lasagna coming out of the oven. Mama would surely come across as the best Italian cook around, because Papa took it upon himself to have his buddy prepare the lasagna. He would make the switch before the tour got to the kitchen, and no one would be the wiser. I was the only other person who knew about this deal, because I had to clue Papa in on the timing and cover for him while he made the switcheroo.

The show proceeded beautifully. "Yes, this is my little sister. Yes, this is a photo of me and Bing Crosby. Here is the piano I practice on. And now we will find Mama in the kitchen. Mama is the best cook in Hollywood. Even Mario Lanza comes here for her lasagna. In fact, it should be coming out of the oven now."

"Ah, *buon giorno*, Mr. Murrow."

"Mrs. Alberghetti, I am told you are a magnificent cook."

"Ah!"

"May we see what you're cooking?"

Anna Maria translated, "Mama, he wants you to open the oven and show the lasagna." The cameras moved forward as Mama Alberghetti opened the oven door. Then all I could hear were screams, and "Mama mia!"s, and some four-letter words that were ten letters in Italian. Mama was in a pure rage. Poor Murrow didn't know what was happening, but Mama had seen instantly that this wasn't her lasagna. Somehow, we managed to get out of that one. I never found out what Mama did to Papa that night.

In those wonderful days when I managed Anna Maria Alberghetti, I kept coming up with new ideas for her. One that particularly struck my fancy was to have this cute little seventeen year old, who sang like an angel and looked like an angel, sponsor a prize fighter. When I first presented the idea to Papa Alberghetti, he almost passed out, but after talking to his buddies about it he warmed to the idea. So I went to Gold's Gym in Santa Monica to find out about the boxing business. Everybody was hyped on a new fighter named Seaman Glass. Seaman was a heavyweight and, believe it or not, a teacher at a local elementary school. He had trouble finding sparring partners because he hit so hard.

Within a few weeks, I'd cut a deal with Seaman Glass's trainer, and Anna Maria Alberghetti had herself a fighter. Seaman's first fight under this arrangement, a six-rounder, was set for the Olympic Auditorium in Los Angeles. I started working on the promotion. We took publicity shots at Gold's Gym, and soon the story had hit sports pages and entertainment sections. I wanted Seaman Glass to look like a heavyweight champ, so I'd ordered him an embroidered bathrobe and shorts and the very latest in Adidas boxing gear. When his opponent walked into the ring, he was wearing a torn and stained T-shirt; his shorts hung down below his knees, and his fly was open.

His shoes seemed to curl up at the toes, and they looked like they were held together with rivets. One shoe had only half a shoelace.

My guy and Mr. Contender met in the center of the ring, looking like Fred Astaire versus Peter Falk, shook hands, and returned to their respective corners. The bell sounded, and they headed towards each other. Seaman was weaving and bobbing and dancing about. The other guy planted his feet on the floor and stared straight ahead. Seaman feigned a left; the other guy barely moved. Suddenly, a gloved fist was shooting directly at Glass's jaw. When it landed, he was airborne: he had more hang time than Michael Jordan. Finally, he crashed to the floor. It took him a couple of hours to wake up, and it took me a couple of months to explain to Papa Alberghetti that you can't win 'em all. Seaman Glass went on to become a prominent writer and journalist in Hollywood.

In the early sixties, I got into concert promotion. I started at the Waikiki Shell in Honolulu. Until then, the Shell had presented mostly amateur and regional shows, but I convinced members of the local chamber of commerce that I could bring in Bob Hope, Frank Sinatra, Dean Martin, and other stars of that caliber. They, of course, were very excited at the prospect. This venture would require important financing, so, once again, I went to see my friend Charlie Mapes. For fifty percent of the profits, Charlie agreed to finance the first concert; three shows—on Friday, Saturday, and Sunday.

Then I went about making good on my promise to reel in the stars. I tried to get Frank Sinatra, Bob Hope, Dean Martin, and Elvis Presley. No luck. My financial guarantee was just too low. The thought then occurred to me that at that point the hottest regular concert attraction was Victor Borge, who had just finished a super-successful engagement at the Golden Theater on Broadway. It was my good fortune that I knew Victor rather well, having been his agent at MCA.

I flew to his farm in Connecticut, where he raised Cornish game hens and minks. In fact, Foopie and Johnny came with me on that trip, and Johnny still remembers the kids' show that Victor put on just for him. As for me, I did one of my all-time great selling jobs: Victor said okay to three days at the Waikiki Shell for the figure the others had turned down.

Elated, I flew to Hawaii to set up the promotion. My first step was to get hold of well-known Honolulu disc jockey Aku Head ("fish head" in Hawaiian). I made an appointment to see him. To get to his office, I had to climb twenty feet up a tree using steps that you could hardly call steps: they were just boards nailed to the tree about twelve inches apart. I felt more like a stuntman than a producer. I ended up making a deal with Aku Head: he would get five percent of the gross in exchange for free airplay and concert advertising. We'd call the show *Cloud Nine*.

We sold out all three concerts. Charlie Mapes was counting his profit, and I was thinking that I'd never made so much money in my life. Borge, on the other hand, was not fazed. He said, "I've sold out every date this year. I knew this would be a sell-out when I agreed to the date." (And I thought it had been my super-selling job!)

The day before the show, a bunch of us were invited by prominent Hawaiian journalist Bill Sherman to a picnic on a nearby island. He had us transported in three small boats. The party included Charlie Mapes; Victor Borge, his wife, his children, and a babysitter; and TV star Hugh O'Brian. We got to the island at noon, had our picnic, and sat back to contemplate life in all of its splendor. As the hours drifted by, Borge kept remarking that the island seemed to be getting smaller and smaller. The rest of us, assuming that it was just Borge being Borge, just laughed heartily. By 3:00 p.m., no one was laughing.

When the boats had dropped us off, the island had appeared to be about nine hundred feet by nine hundred feet—small, but exotic, with one picture-postcard tree rising from its center. Now there was no mistaking it: the island was ten feet by ten feet, and we were huddled around the tree in the middle of what was now a home for Lilliputians. We were assured that this was a natural phenomenon and told not to worry. The boats scheduled to pick us up were nowhere in sight, although a Coast Guard helicopter hovered over our heads. By the time the boats finally arrived, we were knee-deep and I was livid. Bill Sherman and his wife had known about this natural phenomenon, and they presumably thought it was a great joke to play on us civilians.

By the following morning, however, we were back on "cloud nine," sunning ourselves and swimming in the Royal Hawaiian Hotel pool next to Borge's "presidential cabana." As we happily contemplated being sold out for three days (that's seven thousand people a night, for a total of twenty-one thousand tickets), I noticed a disturbance far off on the ocean's horizon. It was as if a wind shear had hit the water a couple of miles offshore. I didn't take it too seriously until, five minutes later, it hit the shoreline. Palm trees bent over double, beach chairs and umbrellas went flying in every direction, and people ran for cover from the pelting rain. It was a veritable typhoon.

Although our dreams for opening night were shattered, we still had two sold-out shows, which, I figured, would allow us to break even. Still, I was devastated. Why had I chosen an open venue like the Waikiki Shell? Why hadn't I opted for the Convention Hall? By midnight, the seas had calmed. The next morning, the weather was beautiful. We had to hire extra box office staff to handle the returns from the canceled show, but everything seemed under control. Still, I couldn't help thinking about the fact that although Charlie was the principal financier, I'd invested all the money I owned in the concert.

Imagine, then, how I felt when this beautiful day ended with another violent storm, which forced us to cancel the second show. The same thing happened on day three: beautiful morning and early afternoon, and then a typhoon. I had not taken out rain insurance— first, because I couldn't afford it, and second, because the chamber of commerce had assured me that there'd be no weather problems at this time of year.

Victor, wonderful man that he was, agreed to take a substantial fee cut, but we still faced a heavy loss. On the third day, Victor said to me, "Pierre, I told you I'd do a show for you, and I will." So, that night, dressed in shorts, Victor took the Waikiki Shell stage in a driving rainstorm and gave his concert. Fortunately, the shell, was a dome-covered structure, and it sheltered Borge and his piano. His audience—Pierre Cossette—sat watching from his seat in the outdoor pavilion, dressed in rain gear worthy of a fisherman, holding a huge pop art umbrella over his head.

Actually, no sooner had Victor made that promise to me than I was on the phone alerting *Life* magazine (the number-one publication in America in 1963) to the possibility of an extraordinary event. A *Life* photographer showed up and captured the moment. Somewhere in my files, I have that picture from *Life*, and I treasure it.

A short time later, Victor called me and said, "Look, I'm going to tour on the West Coast. I'll let you produce some of the dates, which will get back the money you lost in Honolulu. Also, tell Charlie Mapes I'll give him a free night at the Mapes Hotel in Reno." What a terrific human being. Few came better than Victor.

Golf has been part of my life forever. I was raised near Altadena Country Club, and I started caddying there when I was twelve years old. Surprisingly, my parents bought me my first set of golf clubs. They knew I wanted them badly, and one day they took me to Sears

Roebuck and let me pick out my first set. Occurrences like that were rare in our family. I knew I was not the model child, the type who was regularly rewarded for his deeds, and I knew that my parents didn't have a lot of extra money to indulge my whims. Again, this is a memory that I can't square with the bad feelings I carry around about my growing-up years.

Since those days, I've played golf with the best: Bob Hope, James Garner, Sean Connery, Jack Nicholson, Clint Eastwood, Bing Crosby, Dean Martin, Tom Kite, Raymond Floyd, Bruce Litsky, John Miller, Bob Newhart, Andy Williams, Don Rickles, Peter Falk, and many others. My favorite golf tale has to do with James Garner. I was trying to sell a TV musical special to NBC. It was a very tough sell. Finally, J.J. McMahon, the senior exec at NBC, said, "Look, you play golf with all those big stars. Get one of them to do your show." I asked him who he had in mind, and he answered, "I see you playing golf all the time with James Garner. Get him as one of your guest stars, and you have a deal."

Sounded easy enough to me. That weekend I played golf with Jim, and I raised the subject right away. "I'm doing a variety special at NBC, and I'd like you to be a guest star. It pays $7,500. You'll be terrific." Jim said, "I'd love to do it, but I can't sing." Well, I had heard Jim Garner sing before, and I knew this was a cop-out. I didn't get anywhere with him that day, but I invited him to play golf again the next day. Although the top price ever paid for a guest star on a variety show was $7,500, I decided to risk the wrath of my fellow producers and offer him fifteen thousand. He appreciated the offer, but he still insisted that he couldn't sing well enough to be on national television.

After this game, I called my accountant to see whether we dared up the ante by ten thousand dollars. Yet again, I played golf with Jim, and even in the face of my twenty-five-grand offer he wouldn't budge. His answer remained the same: "But I can't sing!" I pushed it up to fifty thousand; it didn't improve his vocal abilities one whit. Crazy with determination, I went back to my accountant. What would happen if I offered the man seventy-five thousand? Could I still break even? We decided to make the show a loss leader. In other words, I'd take the chance of losing money, but I would gain a reputation with the networks for being "a guy who can deliver."

Two days later, I'm back on the golf course with Jim Garner. As you can imagine, by now the man was fed up with my pit-bull persistence. He was doing a slow burn, so I waited until we hit the steam room after the game before I started in on him. There were about five of us in there steaming. All I said was, "Seventy-five thousand." Jim jumped up and, bare-ass naked, belted out the greatest rhythm version of "Day In, Day Out" I'd ever heard.

And so, James Garner, Lee Marvin, and Gene Kelly did my NBC special. I paid Lee the standard $7,500 and Gene, who hosted, twenty-five thousand. The show was great, I was a hero, and I also made a small profit. Mercifully, Jim did not tell Lee or Gene how much he was being paid.

The Egg, a real off-Broadway-type play, was produced by UCLA's dramatic arts program in 1963. Foopie and I saw it and loved it. I immediately recognized it as the perfect vehicle for my comedian client Dick Shawn, who was the Robin Williams of the late fifties and early sixties. I wanted to turn *The Egg* into a musical. I sent a copy of the UCLA version of the play to Dick, and he loved it as much as I did. He, too, saw what could be done with it as a musical, and he agreed to get involved, even though it meant that he'd have to cancel lucrative Las Vegas engagements and concert dates.

I hunted down the playwright, a Frenchman named Felicien

Marceau, in Paris, and I told him I'd love to produce his play on Broadway as a musical starring the hottest American comedian of the day. Although he was flattered that I wanted to produce his work on Broadway, Marceau would not consider turning it into a musical. It didn't help that he'd never heard of the top American composers and lyricists I was recommending to do the music. I stopped the conversation right there.

After some back and forth, Dick and I agreed to go forward with the play as it was, and Marceau was content. Although Dick was basically a song-and-dance man, we rationalized that this role might afford him the chance of becoming a dramatic star. The tough part would be to raise the $120,000 necessary to put on the play. I decided to sell the project piecemeal: one hundred units at twelve hundred dollars apiece. I could write a book about this one showbiz feat alone. Suffice it to say, I came up with one large investor, who purchased four units for $4,800. The other ninety-six investors were in for twelve hundred each. Miracle of miracles, I managed to negotiate successfully with ninety-six investors, ninety-six attorneys, ninety-six business managers, and a lot of agents.

Armed with the money, I now had to make the show happen. I had no contacts on Broadway, but I did know a Los Angeles producer of local plays. His name was Zev Buffman. Zev knew the producing ropes. The next step was to recruit a director. I considered myself very lucky to secure the services of Lamont Johnson, who has since walked away with many awards for his work in television, motion pictures, and theater. Many rehearsals later, we headed for Chicago, and there we opened to rave reviews, including one from one of America's toughest drama critics. Across the street from us was the Broadway-bound production of Tennessee Williams's *Night of the Iguana*. Not only did *The Egg* do better business, but it also won better reviews.

A young Pierre

The Cossette parents in Valleyfield, Quebec

First showbiz venture: Red Skelton performing in Pasadena

Visiting the Old Faithful Inn in Yellowstone National Park, at age 17

With a girlfriend at a USC event

Receiving an award from Bob Hope

Walking the streets of New York City

Pierre's mother with Anna Maria Alberghetti

Ann-Margret and George Burns

On the way to the dressing room with Sammy Davis Jr.

In a production meeting in Las Vegas

The Cossette family dining at Harrah's in Lake Tahoe.
From left to right: Johnny, Dorothy, Andy, a family friend, and Pierre

Harry Cohn, head of Columbia Pictures and Dorothy's boss

ALEC BYRNE

With (from left to right) Don Rickles, Bob Newhart, and Ed McMahon

With Andy Williams and the Chairman of CBS

At a benefit event with first wife Dorothy Foy (seated to the left)

With John Denver

With some Playboy bunnies at a benefit event

The first Malibu home on La Costa Beach

With Michael Landon

With Little Richard and Keith Richards

Golfing with Andy Williams

With Dick Clark

With Dionne Warwick

With Kenny Rogers

With Jerry Lee Lewis and Dick Shawn

Meanwhile, back in New York, theater party orders were pouring in to the Cort Theater, where we were scheduled to open. Dick and I couldn't believe what we'd pulled off. We envisioned ourselves on the cover of *Time*, heralded as the newest, hottest star/producer team on Broadway.

Two days before our New York opening, I was reading Walter Winchell's column. I nearly lost my cookies as I read his pronouncement that Felicien Marceau had been a Nazi sympathizer during World War II. Well, all hell broke loose at the Cort Theater when word got around. All theater parties were canceled, all cash advances were refunded, and we had to paper the house (that is, give tickets away) for opening night. We had great reviews, but we were forced to close after one week.

So, my fame as a Broadway producer was fleeting. Twenty-one years later, I produced *The Will Rogers Follies* on the Great White Way, and it turned out to be the hit that *The Egg* should have been. I was very disappointed with the failure of *The Egg*. I had taken so many risks up to that time—leaving MCA, and putting everything I owned into starting a record company—and all of my ventures had paid off until this debacle. Not only that, but I had asked one hundred close friends for their financial support. They had put up money for me, and I felt that I had let them down.

One day, my receptionist buzzed me to say that a group called the Subtletones was in the lobby and wanted to see me. She said they had musical instruments and gear. I told her that I wasn't interested in seeing a musical group, but she said they were very cute college kids, and I should at least come to the lobby and shake their hands. I went out to see them—three boys and a girl, all as cute as my receptionist had said. One of the boys was wearing a Phi Delta Theta sweatshirt; Phi Delta Theta was my fraternity at USC.

I was all set to send them packing, because I had no intention of getting involved with four college kids. That's the kind of million-to-one shot that doesn't appeal to a sane agent or producer. But these kids were so friendly, so genuine, so interested in the business, that I found myself inviting them to come back at 6:00 p.m., after the doctors and lawyers had left the building. At 6:00, they came into my office carrying a snare drum and a sock cymbal, a stand-up base, and a guitar. The leader, Scott Simpson, walked over to the piano. The girl vocalist, Ann-Margret Olsson, seemed shy.

I was expecting a version of "Over the Rainbow" or "Fools Rush In," but what came at me I couldn't believe. This little girl started shimmying and dancing and strutting; she was shouting out "Come Rain or Come Shine" to a very up-tempo beat. Then she draped herself over my desk, where I was seated, and went for the big finish. I was overwhelmed. I hadn't seen anything like that since Tina Turner. "Where are you from?" I asked. Reverting to her quiet, schoolgirlish demeanor, she said, "Willamette, Illinois." The members of the group were students at Northwestern, and when I asked where they had performed, Ann-Margret said, "at college and school functions and sometimes private parties," adding, "when I was at New Trier High School, I used to sing at the Elks Club on Saturday nights with my uncle."

I asked, "What are you at Northwestern? Sophomores? Juniors? Seniors?"

"We're all juniors," they replied.

"How did you get to Los Angeles?"

"We got into Scott's station wagon and headed to Las Vegas to audition for a summer job."

"What happened?"

"We couldn't find anything. We had eighty-five dollars left, so we decided to come to Los Angeles and find an agent."

"How'd you end up here?"

"Almost everywhere we went, people said, 'You should see Pierre Cossette. He's a talent buyer and also the biggest personal manager in town.' So here we are."

They say that flattery will get you everywhere. I said, "You've come to the right place. I'll try to find work for you. Stick around for two or three days."

The next morning, I called agents Georgia Lund and Joe Rollo. A week later, the Subtletones opened at the Stockman's Hotel in Elko, Nevada. From there they went to the Riverside Hotel in Reno and the Dunes Hotel in Las Vegas. That filled their entire summer. When the rest of the group returned to Northwestern, Ann-Margret stayed behind, because she wanted to be a star.

The problem was, she had very little money and no place to stay. Her parents came out from Chicago to talk the situation over, and she asked me if I would meet with them. I told them that I thought Ann-Margret should graduate from Northwestern before attempting a career, but if she was still adamant about being in show business, she'd have to move to either Los Angeles or New York. The decision came down: Ann-Margret would remain in Los Angeles.

Sincerely believing that this girl was superstar material, I got busy building her career. First, I got her a job at Balboa Island for forty dollars per night, which was twenty dollars below union scale. My next move—an essential one—was to get her an agent. My contacts at MCA were intact, so I set out to get MCA to sign her. I called Jerry Perenchio and Ned Tannen. Jerry was in the acts department, and Ned was in both the television and motion picture departments. (Incidentally, Ned Tannen went on to become president of Paramount, and Jerry Perenchio is now a member of Fortune 500.) I raved to them about this new girl and persuaded them to have lunch with her.

Ms. Olsson, when she wasn't performing, was a very quiet type, and during that lunch she failed to impress Ned or Jerry. I was sure that they would change their minds if they could see her perform, so I convinced them to bring the younger MCA guys together—I'd get the bigwigs—and we'd have one big audition. This would do the trick; MCA would get behind Ann-Margret and make her a star. The audition was held in the MCA Theater, in the MCA office building. The entire agency attended, and it was devastating. She bombed terribly. Jerry and Ned didn't talk to me for six months, and the bigwigs at MCA decided I was crazy.

I had learned from my Las Vegas experience that a star or potential star is not always the best singer, dancer, or actor. Besides possessing an honest combination of talents, a star in the making has to have tenacity. And this girl was tenacious. She knew that the Subtletones didn't have what it took and that she had blown the MCA audition, but she was determined to keep trying. She was going to make it.

At that time, I had booked Rowan and Martin into the Mapes Hotel in Reno. I decided to use this booking as an opportunity to give Ann-Margret her first major job as a solo artist. She would open for Rowan and Martin. Charlie Mapes had a fit. He hated her first performance. He also hated the idea that I managed Rowan and Martin as well as Ann-Margret and was using his place to try out a new kid. He fired her after the first show.

But Ann-Margret and I were undaunted. I took her by the hand and said, "Come on, we're going to Paramount." I sought out Norman Lear and Bud Yorkin, who were producing the Bobby Darin television special on the Paramount lot. Knowing that Ann-Margret did a great impersonation of Bobby singing "Mack the Knife," I thought that if I could get right to the source, I'd land her a job on the show. I knew Bobby, Norman, and Bud quite well—

well enough to persuade them to take time out and watch my new discovery do her impersonation. She did it, and she did it well; however, they all said, "It's too late. You should have called us a few weeks ago."

As we walked off the sound stage, I was feeling pretty dejected, and I muttered to myself, "Another lousy day in show business." Outside, we passed a big sign that said "Jerry Lewis Productions," and I said, "C'mon, Ann, I've got an idea." Having been Jerry's agent at MCA, I had access to him. The receptionist said he was out of town, so I said, "Is Ernie Glucksman in?" Ernie was president of Jerry Lewis Productions. She replied, "Yes, who may I say is calling?" I gave my name, she passed it on, and the next thing she said was, "Mr. Glucksman will see you right away." I'd known Ernie well during my MCA touring days. Telling Ann-Margret to wait for me, I made my way to Ernie's office. After the ritual hellos, I launched into one of my best-ever pitches. I announced that I had discovered a girl who was destined to become a superstar. "Ernie," I continued, "your company should grab this girl, put her under contract, and use her in your movies, TV shows, personal appearances, records—the works. You can sign her exclusively, for peanuts, and she'll make you millions."

As I went on, Ernie kept saying, "Gee, I don't know . . . I'll have to talk to Jerry."

"Talk to Jerry!" I sputtered. "You're the president of this production company, and you have to check with him to sign a contract player? I don't believe it. Where's Jerry, I'll talk to him myself."

"He's in Hawaii."

"Can we get him on the phone?"

"You can try. Here's the number."

I dialed the number and learned that Jerry was on a fishing trip. I still couldn't believe that Ernie wouldn't go for the deal on his own.

A few weeks later, I got a call from Irving Fein, who managed Jack Benny and George Burns. He said, "Pierre, I understand you brought a girl over to see Bud and Norman recently."

I said, "Yes I did. Were you there?"

"No," he answered, "but George Burns was."

"Yes," I said, "I remember he was guesting on Bobby's special. What about it?"

"George wanted me to ask you if you thought she could do a couple of songs and a soft-shoe with George in Vegas."

"Do it?" I responded. "She'd be dynamite!"

So Ann-Margret played the Sahara as part of George Burns's act. That's when the buzz about her really began. And that's why Ann-Margret always says she was discovered by George Burns.

Her next big break was a spot on the Oscar telecast. The Academy Awards were being held at the Santa Monica Civic Auditorium, only fifteen minutes from where I lived. I had invited several prominent show people to my home to watch the proceedings. They were all eager to see Ann's number. Earlier, I'd arranged for her to surprise my guests: twenty minutes after her TV appearance, the doorbell rang, and it was Ann-Margret herself. Everyone was thrilled. Ann performed her Oscar number in my living room at least three times that night.

A year and a half later, Ernie Glucksman called me. He was producing a Jerry Lewis special, and Shirley MacLaine had pulled out. They needed a female superstar.

"Why are you calling me?" I asked.

"For Ann-Margret."

"For Ann-Margret! Ernie, of all the people to call me about Ann-Margret . . ."

He cut in, "Schmuck. I told you I'd get back to you."

I roared with laughter at that one. After Glucksman had turned us down at Paramount, the choo-choo really started rolling. Ann-Margret's first film was *Pocketful of Miracles*, with Bette Davis; she got billing above the title for *Murderer's Row*, starring Dean Martin, and for *Stagecoach*, starring Bing Crosby. She starred in *Bye Bye Birdie*. She costarred with Steve McQueen in *The Cincinnati Kid* and with Elvis Presley in *Viva Las Vegas*—the only movie Elvis ever made for which he shared above-the-title billing.

When you're building a star, you have to think of everything. As I've said, I was dead sure I had a future star on my hands with Ann-Margret Olsson, so one of the things I did early in the game was to call Richard Stolley and Shana Alexander—who were then running the West Coast bureau of *Life* magazine. (Stolley later became editor of *People*, and Shana Alexander is a top journalist.) I told them that they had a golden opportunity to do an interview and photo session with a young unknown performer who would soon hit it big. I worked myself into a frenzy pitching this, and I finally had them believing it. The upshot was that Shana, Dick, and a photographer came to my house to do a shoot with Ann-Margret. Two years later, this photo spread became a four-page before-and-after story in *Life*.

Music Biz

IN THE EARLY SIXTIES, Ann-Margret was set to do Irv Kupcinet's Harvest Moon Ball in Chicago. From there, she would travel to New York to sign a record deal with RCA. I was to accompany her on the trip, and Foopie said she'd drive us both to the airport. She gave Ann a kiss on the cheek when she got out of the car, and Ann started to walk away. I was just saying goodbye to Foopie before catching up with Ann-Margret when I heard a voice behind me say "Pierre Cossette." It was my old high school buddy George Sorenson. I hadn't seen him in a very long time.

George walked along with me, telling me all about how well he was doing. He had built his dad's little shop into a big hardware store and was now clearing two hundred thousand a year. "How about you?" he asked. At that moment we caught up with Ann-Margret, and George said, "Wow, Pierre, you got a great-lookin' daughter."

"George, this is not my daughter. This is Ann-Margret."

George was dumbfounded. "Didn't I just see your wife drop you two off?"

"Yes."

"You're going some place together?"

"Yes, we're going to Chicago and New York."

He scratched his head and said, "Maybe I should have gone into your business." I cut him off: "You'd have to be in showbiz to understand, George. The only difference between us is that your inventory is screwdrivers and lawnmowers and mine is talent—and, in this case, beauty."

In 1963, Columbia released *Bye Bye Birdie*, starring Ann-Margret. Columbia had purchased the Nevin/Kirshner Publishing Company, and as part of the deal, Nevin/Kirchner's best salesman, a young guy named Lou Adler, was given an important job in the music department. He'd be working among all of Columbia's famous composers and musical directors. Adler dressed like a hippie, and the studio's old guard couldn't figure out what he was doing there, but one thing he was doing was visiting the set of *Bye Bye Birdie* and eye-balling Ann-Margret as she worked.

I was still looking for someone to start a record company with, so I approached Lou Adler. Loving the idea of saying goodbye to the Columbia old guard, he agreed to join me, bringing along with him two terrific songwriters: Phil Sloane and Phil Barry. He also enlisted a secretary for them and another for himself. I had to agree to rent a convertible Cadillac for Lou, pay fancy salaries to him and his staff, and, on top of that, put up the cash for producing records. In other words, I was the only investor.

Once again, Foopie was right by my side. To get the record company off the ground, I had to take out loans using our home as collateral and sell stocks and other properties we owned. We put up all the money we had, but Foopie's faith in me didn't waver. We named the company Dunhill Records.

The first thing Lou wanted to do was record Johnny Rivers live from the Whisky A-Go-Go on Sunset Boulevard. We backed a sound truck up to the backstage entrance and recorded six shows in the course of a week. We put Ann-Margret in the "go-go cage," and she was a big hit. Everybody was playing guessing games about the identity of the girl in the go-go cage. Was she part of the show? When I said that Ann-Margret had tenacity, this is what I meant: she was in that cage four hours a night, and she wasn't being paid for it.

Suffice it to say that *Johnny Rivers at the Whisky A-Go-Go* was a number-one hit on record charts worldwide. A single from the album, "Memphis," rocketed to the top of the singles charts. In fact, it was this album that sparked the disco craze.

Soon afterwards, Johnny Rivers asked us to meet a new artist he had met named Barry McGuire. Johnny was a fine person, and Lou and I knew we could trust him, so we set up a meeting with McGuire, who turned out to be the hippest-looking hippie we'd ever seen. Lou agreed to record him, we put him under contract, and his first single, "Eve of Destruction," shot to number one.

Our streak of good luck held. Barry McGuire recommended a new group, the Mamas and the Papas, to us. We had the group rehearse quietly, a cappella, in our office for two or three weeks. Then we went into the studio, and Lou did it again: he produced a worldwide number-one hit album, *If You Can Believe Your Eyes and Ears*. From then on, the group's hits—like "Monday, Monday" and "California Dreamin'"—just kept coming.

At about this time, I took a trip to my birthplace of Valleyfield, Quebec, Canada. My Aunt Thérèse took me around town, introducing me to the mayor, the chief of police, and other local dignitaries. She even arranged for me to have the key to the city, all the while singing my praises as a producer. Aware that none of these people really knew who I was, I felt embarrassed, but she kept babbling on as if I were Cecil B. DeMille and Louis B. Mayer rolled into one.

When we got to city hall, Aunt Thérèse introduced me to a local radio disc jockey, who was waiting there for me. He started speaking to me in French, and I couldn't understand a word he was saying. But, if for no other reason than to live up to my aunt's boasting, I wanted to get across to him that I had produced the world's number-one album for the Mamas and the Papas.

So, in my broken French, I tried to tell him. He then went on the air and started speaking in rapid-fire French. I turned to Aunt Thérèse and asked her what he was saying, only to be told, "He's saying how wonderful it is that you were born in this small Canadian town, went to Hollywood, became a big producer, and the first thing you did was to make a recording with your mother and father." I said, "No! No!" Then I frantically started humming "Monday, Monday" and "California Dreamin'"—but it was too late.

Back at Dunhill, Lou kept the ball rolling. We put out a hit album for Three Dog Night; their single "Joy to the World" was a smash. And on we went with releases by such super acts as Steppenwolf and the Grass Roots. My one disagreement with Lou during that heady period concerned a trumpet player named Dore Alpert. Dore was strictly an instrumental performer, and his concept had to do with bullfights. Lou wanted to sign him. I didn't, and I told Lou, "There hasn't been a hit instrumental act since Louis Jordan and the Tympany Five, and I think it would be a waste of money. My answer is a big no."

Understandably, Dore and his manager, Jerry Moss, felt let down. Then they were pissed off—they'd badly wanted Lou to produce their album, and I had put a stop to it. But they knuckled down and managed to raise enough money to make the album themselves. They changed Dore Alpert's name to Herb Alpert and started their own company, A&M (Alpert and Moss) Records. In 1993, they sold their company for $450 million. No comment.

Before and after we had Johnny, Foopie had one miscarriage after another. We both wanted another baby, so I suggested we adopt. At that time, people in our situation would go to an attorney who would provide them with the names of pregnant women who couldn't keep—or didn't want to keep—their babies. Foopie couldn't face meeting the expectant mothers, so it was up to me. I met many of them before finding one whom I thought was terrific. I liked her and she liked me.

We paid all of her expenses during her pregnancy. When we got the call saying that she was in labor, we dashed to the hospital. It was a boy, and we were thrilled. Foopie felt distressed about taking the baby from his birth mother, so, once again, I was the one who went to meet with the woman. She was crying, and I assured her that we would take good care of her boy. We took baby Andy home from St. Joseph's Hospital in Santa Monica that day in the midst of a wild hail and thunderstorm. I remember it well.

When the time came, we told Andy that he had been adopted, and later we gave him all the relevant papers, encouraging him to look up his biological mother. Andy, who turned out to be six-foot-four and movie-star handsome, chose not to call her then, although eventually he did.

In school, Andy got some bad grades and had some behavioral problems—just like I did—but he did become a fine young man. Although both of my sons were born into the show business life, John was the one who took to it like the proverbial duck to water. Today, he is president of my company. He has turned out to be like me in so many respects that sometimes I find it hard to believe. Andy, although he went deeply into rock and roll as a youngster, had little use for showbiz. He took on some of Foopie's quiet detachment; but he was also a rebel and a protester from the time he was a little boy. I always felt he walked to the beat of a different drummer. You could say it had to do with his being adopted, but then how do you explain the sharp differences between my sister and me? We have the same biological parents. That's why I don't really think it has much to do with genes.

Through Andy's babyhood, Dunhill Records grew tremendously. It became so big that in order to continue we needed major financing. We cut a deal with ABC and brought in a heavyweight to run the company. I'd had lots of fun in the recording and publishing business, but after a while I recognized that I no longer wanted to devote my energies to it. So I sold out, and I never looked back—although I do occasionally think about the $450 million that Jerry Moss got for A&M Records.

In the late sixties, Robert Morse was the star of the Broadway hit *How to Succeed in Business Without Really Trying*. Later, he starred in the movie version. Bobby was a friend of mine, and we had great fun the night the movie opened at New York's Radio City Music Hall. We hired a limo and parked it around the corner from the theater entrance. Having called ahead, we knew what time the screening ended. At that precise moment, we pulled the limo up to the curb; as people poured out of the theater, I jumped from the limo and shouted, "Ladies and gentlemen: Robert Morse." Then Bobby emerged and sang a few bars of "I Believe in You." The looks on people's faces made the whole thing worthwhile. Once they realized that this was really Robert Morse, they rushed the limo to get autographs, but we beat them to it and sped away. We did the same thing three times that night (with stops in between at famous Manhattan watering hole Elaine's).

Back then, my friend Dick Shawn was on fire. People would tell him regularly, "You're the greatest entertainer who ever lived," so I developed a plan to get him into the movies. He didn't need me for the concert and nightclub stuff. I said, "Dick, you've got to come up with a new image. You sing great, but you only use it in a comedic way. If you were to be serious, you'd drive the women crazy. And that's what would get you into motion pictures." I persisted with this idea until Dick finally agreed to open his act with a ballad and sing it straight—but he insisted that he be given protection. "What kind of protection?" I asked.

"Well, if something goes wrong, I want to be able to bail out."

"What do you mean?"

"Get me a stuntman and a stuntwoman, breakaway clothes for the two of them, and a few cases of breakaway champagne bottles," he said.

"Then what?" I asked.

"If the bit isn't working, I'll revert to comedy."

I agreed only because I was certain that he'd finish the opening song and be a big hit. On opening night, I listened as the voice-over announced, "Ladies and gentlemen: the Flamingo Hotel proudly presents the star of our show, Dick Shawn!" Stage right, in a spotlight irised to cover only his face, Dick began singing, "I'm gonna love you, like nobody's loved you, come rain or come shine / Happy together, unhappy together, and won't it be fine." In came the rhythm section, followed by the brass and reeds. Dick was mesmerizing the audience, and I felt like Darryl Zanuck.

The time came for Dick to make his move down into the audience with only his song, a moving spotlight, and a handheld mike. It was pure magic. Then he stopped at the stunt table. "Oh my God," I thought, "what's he doing?" He sang "I'm gonna love you . . ." to the stuntwoman while her stuntman "boyfriend" said, loudly and clearly, "Lay off my chick." Dick kept on singing, ". . . deep as the ocean, high as the mountain . . ." Then I heard, "Hey, I told you to stay away from my chick!" At that moment, I understood that the bit was on and I had been had. The stuntman took the prop champagne bottle (obviously rehearsed) and hit Dick over the head with it. But this so infuriated the guy at the next table that he started punching out the stuntman, who fought back.

In the midst of this free-for-all, you could hear Dick singing his heart out: "The day that you left me / It was just one of those things . . ." Then he began pulling the breakaway clothes off the stuntman and the stuntwoman, and, never missing a note, he threw the girl, now clad only in panties and bra, over his shoulder and walked to the stage, finishing the number in a soaring crescendo.

If you haven't figured it out by now, this business keeps you on your toes. Learning from your mistakes is not an option: it's your ticket to survival. In my early days managing Dick Shawn, I would go with him to various resorts in the Catskill Mountains of New York State, the training ground for all the big-time comedians—Sid Caesar, Red Buttons, Danny Kaye, Buddy Hackett, and many others. Today, new talent auditions at the comedy clubs. In those "mountain" days, a comic would work four or five different clubs a night. After doing his show and grabbing the money, he'd race to the next club.

Dick Shawn did a bit where he would sing "Me and My Shadow," and in the middle of the number he would say, "Hey, Mr. Leader-man, throw me my cane." The orchestra leader would throw the cane, and Dick would grab it in midair; then he'd dance and twirl the cane, tossing it from one hand to the other. I had the job of carrying his cane and collecting the money when he finished his act.

One night, we were driving to a Catskills location. We pulled up to the backstage entrance and went inside. Suddenly, I noticed that I didn't have the cane. I panicked. My mind raced. What had I done with it? Where had I left it? I had to do something fast, before Dick found out. I asked the lone stagehand for a broom, a saw, and some black paint. I set to work sawing off the end the broom and painting the handle black. Luckily, the girl in the box office had a blow dryer, which I borrowed to dry the paint.

By this time, Dick was into his, "Me and My Shadow" routine. I was sweating bullets about my makeshift cane. There was no orchestra leader, so it was up to me to throw the cane from the wings. When the moment came—"Hey, Mr. Leader-man, throw me my cane"—I put a finger on each end of my broomstick cane and threw it to Dick. As always, he caught it, twirled it, and tossed it into his other hand. Visibly startled, he gazed for a moment at his two black hands, but he recovered instantly. Dropping the cane, he got down on one knee, displayed his blackened hands, palms out, to the audience, and broke into a heartbreaking rendition of Al Jolson's "Mammy." It brought the house down, and Dick later included the "Mammy" bit in his regular show.

One aspect of my work as a producer is finding new talent, and it's something I've always enjoyed. In 1969, in a small club in Santa Monica, I caught the act of a comedian by the name of Jud Strunk. He was making twenty-five dollars a night. My years in Las Vegas had taught me what was bad, what was marginal, what was good, what was great. To me, Jud Strunk had it all: the looks, the talent, the attitude. So I went backstage to tell him I was going to make him a star. That's just what I did. His twenty-five dollars a night grew to twenty-five thousand a week; he made a number-one record, and CBS gave him his own TV special.

Here's how it all happened. Jud was a songwriter as well as a comic. As I was well connected in the record business, I was able to get him a record deal. His first effort was "Daisy a Day," and it hit number one on the country charts and made the top five on the pop charts. Armed with this success, I arranged a meeting with Marvin Koslow, chairman of the board of Bristol Myers's advertising and marketing division. My concept was to take this unknown and allow him to be "discovered" nationally with his own TV special, sponsored by Bristol Myers. The company would then have the option to sponsor a Jud Strunk weekly variety show. Koslow had never heard of Jud Strunk. Neither had the general public, except record buyers, but record buyers represented only a dot on the landscape of the mass audience. I persuaded Marvin to catch Jud's act in Maine. Maine, Vermont, and Massachusetts were Jud's best showcases. Fans loved him there, and I knew his act would come off well.

So, Marvin Koslow, his assistant, two other people from Bristol Myers, Merrill Grant (head of the Bristol Myers account for Grey Advertising), and I flew from New York to Farmington, Maine, in a Bristol Myers jet. Merrill had me in a death grip for the entire trip. "How could you put Grey in this position?" he demanded. "You should have come to me first, not Koslow. Now I'm in the position of having to recommend, or not, a TV special for a guy nobody's ever heard of."

I told him not to worry, that I had great faith in this guy. As we landed, we could see that a crowd of several hundred people had gathered. Marvin said, "This guy must be hot. Is that crowd for him?" Later I learned that the crowd had come to see a jet plane land—a first for Farmington. From that high we sank to a real low—at least I did. As we walked down the runway, we could hear music. A four-piece band was there to greet us. On banjo was Strunk. I was beside myself. Koslow had come expecting to see a future star, not a banjo picker in a local band. I ran ahead and ordered Jud to get the hell out of there.

We checked in to the local hotel, which was like a rundown Holiday Inn. I was worried, but Merrill Grant was close to a nervous breakdown. He was convinced that Grey was going to lose the account for being part of this "amateur night in Dixie" scheme. The clerk told us that Mr. Strunk was expecting us in the conference room for a reception. The "conference room" turned out to be twenty-five feet square, at most. On a card table were a bottle of scotch, a bottle of vodka, a bottle of gin, a dozen plastic cups, and a salad bowl filled with ice. Jud had invited a few other guests, and one of them had a real fish sticking out of his back pocket; another, a six-foot redhead in heavy makeup, was clearly the town hooker. As Merrill Grant headed to the bathroom to throw up, I explained to Marvin all about Jud's unique personality.

Considering that I had tried to convince Marvin that Jud Strunk was an artist who could fill arenas and was widely known among young people, things were not going well. And, as I told myself, reminding him that Elton John was a big concert attraction long before the mass audience had heard of him probably wouldn't help much. As if all this wasn't enough, Koslow was assuming that Jud's concert would be staged in a local ball field, which could accommodate an audience of six thousand to ten thousand. I no longer knew what to think.

We followed Jud's pickup truck to the concert. Koslow and Grant were used to stretch limos, and here we were packing ourselves into a rented Chevy, which I would drive. Grant climbed in beside me. I decided that he was maneuvering himself into position to kill me. Remember, I had no idea where Jud was leading us. I knew that it wouldn't be a ballpark or a four-thousand-seat stadium; however, since Jud was at least a local celebrity, I figured that it would be someplace decent. When Jud stopped in front of a market and called to us "Let's go!" I was stunned. To the right of the market was a door that led to a basement nightclub. Down we went. The place could hold an audience of sixty-five, including me, Koslow, and a now-comatose Merrill Grant.

Marvin, I have to say, was slow to react, but by now he, too, was taking a burn to all of this. I'm sure he envisioned being accused of improper use of the corporate jet, even though he was president. His occasional glances at me suggested that he was not amused. But Merrill Grant didn't hold back, whispering loud in my ear, "You cocksucker!" And then it happened.

From a sound system borrowed from the Kiwanis Club came, "Ladies and gentlemen, Jud Strunk!" For the next hour, Jud mesmerized the audience the way I knew he could. The result of all this was that a Jud Strunk special aired on CBS prime time, "brought to you by Bristol Myers." Although I did have to recruit Andy Griffith and others as guest stars, it was the first time a major network had aired a TV special featuring a complete unknown.

Following my success with Strunk on CBS, Bristol Myers changed their policy on weekly shows, so I tried to sell Chevrolet one featuring Jud. My first call was to Tom Adams, chairman of Campbell-Ewald, which represented Chevrolet. When I told him about my idea for a Jud Strunk weekly show, he said he'd never heard of Jud Strunk. I offered to fly Jud in to meet him. We agreed to meet Tom after an annual event at the Masonic Temple in Detroit, at which he was being honored. Tom would send me two tickets to the event. He also supplied me with his home address, saying, "If Jud is as good as you say he is, have him bring his banjo to my house after the event to sing a few songs."

Three thousand people had gathered at the Masonic Temple. The Redford High School band, marching straight down the center of the hall, delivered the event's grand finale. As I watched the band, an idea formed in my producer's brain. I left Jud and ran down to catch the bandleader, a middle-aged schoolteacher. I said, "How'd you like to make a thousand dollars to buy sheet music and music stands for your band?"

He said, "I'd love it."

I said, "Okay, I'll give you one thousand dollars if you follow me to Bloomfield Hills with your band."

"Then what?" he asked.

"Then the kids get out of the buses and walk slowly and quietly to a place in front of a house. I'll go to the door, and when it opens I'll turn around and give you a cue. Have the band play ninety seconds of 'I Wish I Were in Dixie' and then run like hell for the buses and get out of there."

I explained that I was in show business, so I knew what I was doing—that the house belonged to Tom Adams, chairman of Campbell-Ewald, that their performance would make headlines, and so forth. The bandleader was equally impressed that I owned Dunhill Records, as were all the kids. He had me explain the master plan and strategy to the kids, and they loved it. It was very late by the time we got organized.

I was in the lead car with Jud Strunk. Behind us were four busloads of kids and two instrument-carrying trucks. We arrived at 1:00 a.m. One hundred and seventy-one kids, quiet as mice, took up their positions behind a hedge in front of Tom's mansion. Not one neighbor was awakened. Jud and I went to the front door and rang the bell. Tom answered in his pajamas, obviously pissed that we were so late. I turned and gave the band its cue. The band members stood up as one and blasted "I Wish I Were in Dixie" like it had never been played before. After ninety seconds, they stopped abruptly and ran for the buses. They were out of there in five minutes.

Now the street was filled with pajama-clad residents wondering what the hell was going on. Someone had called the police. The fire department was there. Tom was still in shock. Jud and I were taking it all in, listening to the complaints, and the police saying, "What brass band?" and the firemen saying, "Did anybody see a brass band?"

When they'd all left, I looked at Tom sheepishly. He blurted out, "You son of a bitch! People could have been killed here tonight!" I said, "No way—it's just show business, and, by the way, Jud would like to do a few routines and songs on his banjo." We left Tom Adams's house at 3:30 a.m.

The next day, as I had predicted, our previous night's exploits made headlines in all the Detroit papers. I still have the clippings in my files, and once in awhile, if I want a good laugh, I take them out. Jud went on to headline in Lake Tahoe and Las Vegas. I know that he would have made it to superstardom if it weren't for his daredevil personality. Early in his rise to fame, he bought an airplane, learned to fly it, and was killed in it soon after.

The Grammys

ALTHOUGH I SOLD DUNHILL in 1966, it was the record business that got me into the Grammy Awards. In 1969, I went to the National Academy of Recording Arts and Sciences and offered to buy the rights to televise the Grammy Awards live.

At that point, I was partners with Burt Sugarman in what we called the CoBurt Corporation. My association with Burt started when I sold him on the idea of putting up ten thousand dollars for an option on a book I thought would make a great movie. As those things often go, the project languished, and Burt got nervous about his investment. Eventually, I wrote him a check for the ten thousand, and we went on to do good business together.

Burt was a tough, take-no-prisoners kind of businessman. I was the total opposite. He had heavyweight contacts in the advertising world, and, with my experience in producing, he thought we should do TV specials together. I would come up with the ideas, and he would sell them. In fact, my short stint with Burt marked my first venture into television.

Working in television, I found that my years of experience in the variety business served me well. Back then, some of the top TV shows were having a tough time lining up guest stars. *The Andy Williams Show* and *The Glen Campbell Show* not only competed with each other for stars, but they also competed with *Perry Como, Dean Martin, Carol Burnett, The Colgate Comedy Hour*, and many others. I had seen a young singer named Jose Feliciano perform, and I was certain he would make it big. After he made his first recording, "Light My Fire," I called his manager, George Grief, and asked him if he'd like Jose to star in his own special. He thought I was kidding, but I had a scheme. Because Jose was blind, he couldn't move easily around the stage, so I said, "We'll build a set in the shape of a big cross, and we'll position Jose at the center. He stays there, and the guest stars will walk along the four arms of the cross to join him. The audience will be seated at tables situated in the four spaces formed by the cross."

George said, "Great, now how do you get guest stars?" I told him that I'd guarantee that Jose would do four guest appearances for Andy Williams's TV season and four for Glen Campbell's. Because Feliciano wasn't that well known, those shows wouldn't have to pay the big bucks, and that would make them happy. And Feliciano would benefit from a lot of exposure. In return, Andy and Glen would appear on Jose's special. It was a fabulous way for George to launch his performer. He could see that, and he said, "If you can do it, great. I heard you were a miracle worker."

So I got Andy and Glen for Jose's special, and then, due to my relationship with Dionne Warwick and Burt Bacharach, I was able to make the same deal with them: Jose would guest on their specials, and they would guest on his. We now had the four hottest recording acts in the country performing as guests on a single special. We called the show *Feliciano Very Special*. It was a huge success.

That led to a few more specials. Burt managed to sell *Switched On Symphony* to Bell Telephone. It was an extension of the show I had done for Jimmy Durante and Helen Traubel, as well as the Anna Maria Alberghetti symphony show we'd done in Las Vegas. The idea was simple: we would combine Zubin Mehta, the Los Angeles Philharmonic, and four young virtuosos from the classical world with four breakthrough rock acts: Santana; Emerson, Lake, and Palmer; Jethro Tull; and Ray Charles.

When I first set this up, I met with the conductor of the Los Angeles Symphony Orchestra, Zubin Mehta, and the president of the Los Angeles Philharmonic, Ernest Fleishman. I presented to them the idea of having the Los Angeles Symphony (118 musicians strong) perform with several pop and rock acts and an equal number of young classical concert virtuosos—all under Mehta's baton. At the time, it was a crazy idea, but I delivered an impassioned pitch for it, and I won.

The people from Bell Telephone who attended the rehearsal the day before the taping were shocked to see twenty-five groupies for every participating rock band, and more groupies for those twenty-five groupies. Also, each of the bands' sidemen had his own limousine. The sound stages of NBC had never seen anything like it. An hour before air time, the bands got together and had an unbelievable jam. The classical kids jumped in where they could. One of the bits we'd planned was to have a violinist hit a clinker, one beat ahead of everyone else. The camera would pick up a scowl on the face of Zubin Mehta and then pan to the errant violinist, Jack Benny. That was the whole bit. We did it, and it was hilarious.

I later learned that before the show, as the limos were pulling up to the stage entrance and dropping off the rockers and their entourages and instruments, a nondescript Chevy sedan arrived and parked in one of the spaces reserved for limos. A lone gentleman stepped out and, reaching into the back seat, extracted a violin case. He then proceeded to lock the car and walk towards the stage door, violin case in hand. The man was Jack Benny. When people ask me how the business has changed, I always remember Jack Benny. The old-timers traveled alone; newer generations travel en masse.

The Los Angeles Symphony Association was so thrilled at the success of this television special that Mrs. Norman Chandler decided to throw a banquet in my honor. When I showed up, there were three hundred people milling around, and I couldn't spot a single person I knew. I didn't even know my hostess. Finally, I saw a familiar face in that black-tie crowd. I couldn't think of his name, nor could I recall who he was, but it didn't keep me from going over to him and starting a friendly conversation. After I'd chatted with him for about ten minutes, I saw my lawyer, Dick Harris, making a beeline towards me.

"What are you doing?" Dick said, pulling me aside. "Mr. and Mrs. Chandler are really pissed off."

"Why?" I said.

"Why? Because you haven't said hello to them yet, and you're standing here talking to the maitre d'."

"The maitre d'?"

"Yes, he's from Chasen's. Chasen's is catering the party."

I always was a good tipper. Anyway, the show was a complete smash, and Burt and I became the fair-haired boys of Bell Telephone and Grey Advertising. They dearly wanted to do a Simon and Garfunkel special; they'd tried and failed many times to pull it off. This duo was hot, and they were almost impossible to get for television. But, given my record company connections and the fact that their manager was a friend of mine, I had a shot. And I pulled it off.

We went into production in New York. Charles Grodin, the actor-turned-talk-show-host, was the head writer for the show, along with Paul Simon and Art Garfunkel. Paul came in and played the opening song he had just written for the special. It was awful and absolutely wrong for the high-spirited show I was trying to produce. We argued. I did not want to start the show that way, but Paul was insistent. He refused to write a new song to replace it. We got to the point where our differences were, as they say in legal circles, "irreconcilable." Simon and Garfunkel paid me off and hired another producer.

Two years later, I was producing the Grammy Awards telecast for the second year running. Simon and Garfunkel's "Bridge over Troubled Water," the lousy song I had refused to include in the special, won everything: Best Song, Best Record, and so on. To this day, whenever I run into Paul Simon he'll say, "Hey, Pierre, I've got a new song I'd like you to hear. I'd like your opinion." And we have a good laugh.

After CoBurt got Simon and Garfunkel, Bell Telephone must have decided we could move mountains. They asked us to get the Beatles, at the time the most successful recording act in the world. I told Bell we'd try, but only if they armed us with a firm deal. They did. In fact, it was then the largest license fee ever given for a television show.

Alan Klein, lawyer for the Beatles, was a man I knew well. When I called to tell him I wanted the Beatles for a TV special, he said, "What's new? The whole world wants the Beatles for a television special." But I made such a fervent pitch that Klein finally arranged for us to meet the group in London, at the offices of Apple Records.

So Burt and I headed off to London. We checked into the Hyde Park Hotel, a beautiful establishment right across the street from a beautiful lake in an equally beautiful park. I got up early, crossed the street, bought a couple of bags of popcorn, and rented a rowboat. Cruising out into the middle of the lake, so peaceful, so quiet, I shared my popcorn with the ducks and left the cares of show business behind me. Then I was shaken out of my reverie by what sounded like the mating call of a bull moose. It was Burt Sugarman shouting at the top of his lungs, "We're meeting the Beatles in half an hour! What are you doing?" I had lost track of the time. God how I wish I had a video of the people watching Burt scream, "We're meeting the Beatles!"

We got to Apple Records and were escorted into an office, where Paul McCartney, George Harrison, John Lennon, and Ringo Starr were waiting to meet us. I gave them the pitch of the century, promising to produce a fantastic TV special. I had them mesmerized, or so I thought. Even Sugarman thought I was winning them over, but one by one they slowly peeled off until only Ringo was left. I ended my pitch with graphics, and Ringo said, "Look, lads, I'd be happy to see the tapes you brought." We showed our tapes to Ringo, and he seemed to like what he saw.

And he liked us enough to invite us to stay at his house. Ringo's home was very simple; the furniture was what you'd expect to see in a farmhouse. His wife, Maureen, cooked us up a great dinner, and we asked a million questions about the Beatles. Many of our questions sent Ringo to *The Beatles Book*, which was chock-full of Beatles history. It seemed odd to us that he should have to look up the answers.

We returned to L.A. the next day, but in spite of Ringo's warm hospitality, we were going home empty-handed. A year later, Ringo came to L.A., and he called me. Foopie and I took him to dinner at Matteo's, the popular show biz watering hole in Westwood. After dinner, as we were waiting for our car, Gary Morton came out and pulled me back into the restaurant. "Pierre, what the fuck's the matter with you? Lucille was sure you'd bring Ringo over to our table so she could meet him." Gary, of course, was married to Lucille Ball. I said, "Okay. Sorry. I'll bring him back in."

I told Ringo we had to go back inside and say hello to Lucille Ball. "Who's Lucille Ball?" he asked. I explained to him that she was America's hottest comedian, adding, "Haven't you seen *I Love Lucy*?" He said he hadn't, but he agreed to meet her if I wanted him to. So we went to talk to Lucy and Gary, and they were delighted. On the way home, I said, "Ringo, how can you not know Lucille Ball?" He replied, "Look, old chap. I've only spent three days in America in my life, including this one. I guess we sell so many records that everybody knows us, but that doesn't mean we know everybody." That made sense to me.

Through this personal contact, I was able to get the Beatles to be presenters at the Grammy Awards. Each Beatle appeared on a different Grammy show, and one time three of them showed up together. Even in a presenter capacity, they were big box office.

The Prime Time Access ruling came along in 1971, and it changed the course of television history. Prime-time network hours were 7:30 p.m. to 11:00 p.m., and they applied to the major networks: ABC, CBS, and NBC. The ruling simply meant that the 7:30 p.m. to 8:00 p.m. time slot had to be given back to local stations to program in accordance with the interests of their viewers. Because local stations couldn't afford expensive programming, the time slot was used mostly for cooking shows or chamber of commerce panel talk shows. The stations owned and operated by the networks fared a little better, but the networks were only allowed to own five stations each. The networks owned stations in New York, Los Angeles, and Chicago, as well as in two other large Neilson-ratings cities.

At about that time, my friend Jerry Frank brought me an idea for a patriotic show featuring a band and eighteen singers and dancers; the host would be Johnny Mann. Jerry called it *So Proudly We Hail*. It looked good to me, so I called the CBS-owned station in

L.A. and asked the manager to come and see a rehearsal. The deal was set up by my old friend Bob Wood, who had been the local station manager but was then president of CBS. After the audition, I asked the manager, "Would you program this in the 7:30 p.m. to 8:00 p.m. slot if I brought you a sponsor?" He said yes.

Burt Sugarman, who was still my partner, had Detroit contacts with General Motors and their advertising agency, Campbell-Ewald. The people at Campbell-Ewald were interested in sponsoring *So Proudly We Hail*, but first they wanted to see the show on its feet. We hired a bus and took the show to the Sahara Hotel in Las Vegas, where we put on a full performance for the Campbell-Ewald people. Since it was a freebie, we were able to get a large audience, but we also added personnel from the Nellis Airforce Base. And because we set the whole thing up as an audition for the Sahara Hotel people, they paid for most of the mounting and stagehand expenses.

The Campbell-Ewald people were very impressed, but they weren't willing to buy a weekly series. They told us, however, that if we got enough big-name guest stars for a TV special and a network to program it, they would buy some time on the special. We cast the show with superstars like Henry Fonda, Pearl Bailey, and Gene Kelly, and we did the show at ABC studios. It aired, and it was a hit on all three fronts: ratings, reviews, and audience reaction. We changed the name from *So Proudly We Hail* to *Johnny Mann's Stand Up and Cheer*, and it went into syndication as the very first original prime-time access show designed for the 7:30 p.m. to 8:00 p.m. time slot.

That success, which lasted for four years, opened up the time slot all over the country. Someone once said to me, "Pierre, you didn't start original programs for prime-time access syndication. *The Lawrence Welk Show* and *Hee Haw* were on before you." Wrong! Those shows weren't originals; they had been network hits, and they were not in the prime-time access slot.

For the Grammy Awards deal, Burt and I had agreed to split the option cost of $125,000 fifty-fifty. (In today's dollars, that $125,000 would be closer to $1,250,000.) We both thought it was a terrific concept. With my experience in the record industry, I was certain I could land the rights. I was right. What I did not know was that none of the three networks had an iota of interest in airing the Grammy Awards. It was a time when networks didn't want anything to do with longhaired counterculture hippie types. That $125,000 investment, which I thought was the best deal I'd ever made, soon became the worst deal I'd ever made. NBC had zero interest. "If we'd had interest, we wouldn't have dropped *The Best on Record*," they said. *The Best on Record* was a taped show that had been televised, piece by piece, in different locales and aired three months after the actual Grammy Awards. In other words, it was not a live event. And CBS and ABC said, "If it was a good deal, then why did NBC drop it?"

It was one of the toughest deals I've ever been involved in. I just couldn't get it off the ground, and the option would expire soon. Finally, I received a glimmer of hope from ABC. "If you can deliver Frank Sinatra, Dean Martin, or Andy Williams to host the show," they said, "we will program the Grammy Awards." But, even for me, this seemed like a near impossible feat. Sinatra was the hottest guy in show business, and Dean Martin and Andy Williams were at the peak of their television careers. With time running out, I put all of my efforts into Andy Williams. I knew Andy well enough to understand that he would not want to host the show, but I stayed on him and drove him crazy. Finally, he said yes—and that's how the live Grammy Awards got on the air.

We did the show from the Hollywood Palladium, and it was a tremendous success. Once again, I felt like Rocky Balboa. My deal with ABC and the Recording Academy was to rotate the show every year from Los Angeles to New York to Nashville. So, after our Hollywood triumph, we went to New York. Once again, the telecast was a success. The following year, we were scheduled to do the show from Nashville. However, ABC had negotiated a one-year deal with six one-year options, and a few weeks before the option date was up, an ABC exec called me and said, "We do not want to televise the show from Nashville. We'll only do it from New York or Los Angeles." Naturally, I had to ask why. This was the answer: "We don't feel you can get the big recording stars to go to Nashville, and it will become a country show, which we don't want. But we'll definitely pick up the option if you agree to New York or Los Angeles."

I went to Christine Farnon, who was then executive director of the Recording Academy, and Glen Rose, who was its president. Glen lived in Nashville and was a major domo of country music. No way was he going to give in to ABC's edict. I never believed that ABC would follow through and drop the Grammy Awards. That's the main reason I didn't knock myself out trying to persuade Glen. The option date came, and I was flabbergasted when ABC dropped the show. I couldn't believe it. My lawyer, Dick Harris, called to remind me that with ABC out of the picture, I had only sixty days to pick up the option I had with the Recording Academy to do the show from Nashville. If I didn't do it, the rights would revert to the academy.

Sixty days passed, and, as hard as I tried, I could not strike a deal anywhere. Then I surprised everyone by picking up the option myself. This meant, very simply, that I was guaranteeing to televise the 1973 Grammy Awards, with or without a network. I still had several months to sell NBC or CBS on it. If I failed in that attempt, I could get the show onto syndicated television, but I knew that by doing so I'd lose a fortune.

In desperation, I went back to NBC. Their answer was immediate and to the point: "ABC just dropped it. We didn't want it when we had it, and we don't want it now." My only hope, then, was Bob Wood, the president of CBS. I had known Bob since college days, and I could level with him. I said, "Look, Bob, I'm in real trouble. I've picked up the Grammy Awards on my own, and if I don't get a network to program it, I'm going to lose a fortune. You've got to help me." He told me that he'd do what he could, but he wasn't hopeful.

For a full week, I kept after Bob. He finally said, "Look, Pierre, I'd like to help you out, but I'm not running a one-man store here. All my salesmen and programming guys know that ABC didn't pick up the option, and you then went to NBC, and they also turned you down. I can't buck those kinds of odds. If ABC and NBC had it and didn't want it, the only answer I can give you is no. It hurts, but that's the answer."

It was a Friday, and I had a 7:00 p.m. flight to Los Angeles. I was at 21 having lunch when I ran into Bob Wood's wife, Laurie. She said, "Pierre, how are you? What's going on? What are you doing in New York?"

"I came in on business. I'm going back to Los Angeles at 7:00."

"Oh," she said, "you can't do that. You've got to spend the weekend with us. I'm going home at 4:30; please say you'll come with me. You'll be there when Bob comes home from work. What a great surprise for Bob."

"Okay," I said.

As I write this, I'm again feeling the thrill of that moment . . . "a great surprise for Bob" was a gross understatement. When Bob came home, he had Laurie, the kids, and me waiting for him. After having spent five consecutive days hounding him about the Grammy Awards, I'd shown up at his house on the very day he thought he had finally gotten rid of me. Of course, I continued to pester him all day Saturday and Sunday. I knew he was wishing I'd drop dead. By Sunday night, I had to admit defeat.

On Monday morning, I was set to go into the city with Bob; he'd arranged for his driver to deliver me to the airport. At 6:30 a.m., I got up to go to the bathroom, and I noticed that Bob and Laurie's bedroom door was ajar. Acting on a wild impulse, I walked into their room, climbed into bed between them, and threw a leg over Laurie. (You have to understand that I knew both of them very well, and I knew that Laurie had a terrific sense of humor.) "What the hell are you doing?" Bob said.

"Look Bob," I answered, "if you don't give me a date for the Grammy Awards, I'm going to do to Laurie what ABC did to me. We shouted back and forth, and all the time Laurie was roaring with laughter. At last Bob yelled, "Okay, I'll buy your fuckin' show, just get off my wife and get out of my bed!"

We took the Grammys to Nashville, and the show was a smash. We got name people, and we got a fifty-one share of the audience; in short, we did all the things that ABC said we wouldn't be able to do. Bob Wood became a hero for taking such a high-risk proposition and making it work. I later heard that at ABC they went bananas over the dumb decision they'd made. Their response was to call Dick Clark and ask him to set up a competing show. He did. It was *The American Music Awards*, which, I hardly need tell you, has been highly successful for years.

Dick had an easy go of it. He could pick all the hits and the hit performers without restriction. But on the Grammy Awards, we could only allow that year's nominees to perform, and that sometimes created problems. A perfect example was Neil Diamond and Barbra Streisand's duet "You Don't Bring Me Flowers." It was a number-one hit, but we couldn't include it in the Grammys telecast because its release date was two days later than our cutoff date. Neil and Barbra were not amused. The following year, when the song was no longer on the charts, Neil and Barbra were nominated, and they did perform it. This, unfortunately, has happened a few times, but I established that policy for a reason, and I can live with it.

After the second year, I was able to buy out Burt Sugarman and take over the entire Grammy Awards show. But I should say that those years with Burt were two of the most adventurous of my life in show business. By the time Burt and I parted company, we could look back on some great shared achievements. Burt is now an enormously successful financier, and he's married to *Entertainment Tonight*'s Mary Hart. I went on to do prime-access shows for Procter & Gamble: *Sha Na Na*, *The Andy Williams Show*, and *The Glen Campbell Show*. In addition, I did *Sammy and Company*, starring Sammy Davis Junior, which became a successful variety/talk show for ABC, and *Salute*, starring Dick Clark, for Universal.

I had a difficult time selling the Sha Na Na weekly series to Procter & Gamble. The company didn't like the group's image: bikers in black leather with chains hanging all over them. I had to fly to Cincinnati to convince a hostile group of Procter & Gamble executives that Sha Na Na was really like a cartoon—larger than life, but basically harmless and lots of fun. Since I'd be meeting with twenty-two Proctor & Gamble people, I brought along twenty-two cellophane-wrapped Sha Na Na albums. What I didn't know was that on the album's inside jacket was a photo of the group, in their leather and chains, with a big sign that said "We're Gonna Bust Some Ass."

One executive held it up and said, "Mr. Cossette, is this what you call 'lots of fun'?" Somehow I tap-danced my way out of that one, and an hour later I scored a sale. Fortunately, it turned out to be a tremendously successful prime-access show. Not only did *Sha Na Na* run for 156 shows, it was a leader in the prime-access boom that followed.

At the beginning, I was the only one doing original programming for prime access. Later, the competition for the prime-access time slot became fierce. Universal, Paramount, Disney, MGM, Time-Warner, Twentieth Century Fox, Viacom, and a host of others developed big departments for this type of syndicated programming, and the dream spot has remained 7:30 p.m.

Getting into the syndication business was a turning point for me. After I sold Dunhill Records, I had continued to second-guess myself. Had I done the right thing? But now I knew that I'd made the right move. I was into something that I really loved doing. Actually, our lives went through a sea change after I sold Dunhill. I got a call from Marvin Meyer of major Hollywood law firm Rosenfeld, Sussman, and Meyer. At that time they represented Marlon Brando, Julie Andrews, and Jimmy Stewart, to name a few. Marvin said to me, "Pierre, we have a golden opportunity here, and we want you to be part of it. We want to buy General Artist Corporation [next to the William Morris Agency, the most powerful entertainment agency in town]. We've put together the financial package, and we want you to be president and CEO. You can invest as much or as little as you want—no matter. We'll give you an equity position with stock options. Interested?" I happened to know that Herb Siegel owned GAC and that he was negotiating to buy Paramount Pictures. The Justice Department had told him that he couldn't own a talent agency and a movie studio at the same time—he had to be a buyer or a seller—so he wanted out of GAC and in to Paramount. (The same thing had happened to Lew Wasserman when he wanted to buy Universal Studios. He had been forced to sell MCA.)

Well, Marvin's offer was a shocker. I had left the agency business when I was making thirteen thousand a year, and here I was, ten years down the road, invited to be CEO of what was arguably the largest talent agency in the world. Things were going great, I was on target with what I wanted to do in my professional life, and now this! Foopie and I talked it over, and I decided to do it. So I called Herb Siegel and said, "Herb, I want to buy GAC." He said, "That's a wonderful move for you. But I'm out of it. You have to call Larry Barnet, my chief executive. He's in charge of the transition."

I said "Thanks" and hung up. I hadn't mentioned to Marvin that Larry Barnet had been my immediate boss at MCA when I was making that thirteen thousand a year. It was a good thing I had Marvin Meyer backing me up, because even though Larry knew I was doing well, any offer from me to buy GAC without Meyer's name behind it wouldn't have been taken seriously. Anyway, we started a series of meetings with the principals at GAC—all six of them. Each had a stake in GAC and had to be kept in the fold. We met on the West Coast and on the East Coast.

A condition of our offer was that we be permitted to examine all of GAC's books and records. No one at GAC had yet said, "We want X amount of dollars"; they only wanted to sell. After going back and forth for a few months, Marvin and I grew weary—and wary. As it turned out, the principals were arranging their own financial package with which they would fare much better than they would have through an arrangement with a third party, like me. GAC eventually became ICM. I think about that sometimes, but for the most part I look upon it as just another day in show business.

Andy Williams is perhaps my best friend. I've known him for years. Somewhere along the line, I nicknamed him Pussy, and that is what I always call him. When people ask us how he got the name, neither of us can answer—we just don't remember.

I decided to give a party on a Saturday, and my brand new secretary was handling the invitations. Andy was in Australia, so I didn't invite him, but then I spoke to someone on the Friday who said that Andy was due back the next day, the day of my party. I was delighted. So, before I went to lunch, I left a note on my secretary's desk asking her to get hold of Andy and invite him to the party. When I returned, she was in tears, almost hysterical, in fact.

I said, "What's the matter?"

Sobbing, she said, "You're such a nice man, and you have such a nice family, and I want to work here, but I just can't do what you asked. The only person I know is an airline stewardess . . . she gets around a lot, but I just can't ask her that."

Baffled, I said, "What in God's name are you talking about?"

She handed me back the note I had left. It said, "Get Pussy for the party." Sometimes I just don't think.

Years later, I was at 21 in New York, a bastion of maleness at that time, and I was sitting at the bar. Suddenly, in walked Andy. I hadn't seen the guy in six months, and, again without thinking, I whipped around on my stool and called out "Pussy!" Well, Andy kept right on walking. Not a hint of recognition for his old buddy. All eyes turned towards me. I wanted to crawl quietly away.

Speaking of my friend Andy, he once told me a great story about his dad, Jay Emerson Williams. Williams Senior was a barbershop quartet kind of guy and a big champion of his kids, whom he had trained to sing. The boys formed an act. The family lived in Iowa, and the Williams Brothers did pretty well locally. Their dad decided that the time was right to get them an agent. Someone gave him the name of Lee Shapiro, and he headed for New York to talk to the agent about representing the Williams Brothers. The boys had wanted to give their dad a good-luck token, so before he left they'd presented him with a tie clip engraved with his initials. Jay Emerson Williams walked into Lee Shapiro's office and sat down. On his tie clip were the initials "J.E.W." Lee Shapiro took one look and said, "I'm proud too, but isn't that a bit much?"

Miami hosted the Super Bowl in 1976. I was producing *Super Night at the Super Bowl*, hosted by Jackie Gleason and Andy Williams, and starring Joe Namath, Bob Newhart, Burt Reynolds, and Dinah Shore. Pulling it all together hadn't been easy. (But when is it ever easy?)

When I called Bob Newhart to ask him to be a guest star, he said, "Pierre, I'd do anything for you, but your show is on Saturday night in Miami and I'm working at the studio until 8:00 on Friday night. Sorry." When I called Burt Reynolds, it was the same thing. And Dinah Shore, same thing. So I called my friend Bob Anderson, who was chairman of Rockwell International and a guy who loved show business. I said, "Bob, you not only make those Saberliner jets, but you also fly one, right?" Bob said he did and asked me why I wanted to know. I said, "How would you like to fly Burt Reynolds, Bob Newhart, and Dinah Shore to Miami for the Super Bowl? I also have a great pair of fifty-yard-line tickets for you."

Without hesitation, Bob agreed, and believing that I'd solved the logistics problem, I called Bob Newhart, Burt Reynolds, and Dinah Shore again. "I'll send limos to pick you up at 8:00 p.m. and take you to the airport to fly to Miami via private jet." Pow! I nailed them. I was at the Miami airport when the plane landed. Newhart got off first, and he gave me a dirty look. Reynolds followed him and gave me a dirtier look. Then sweet Dinah Shore got off and gave me a dirty look. Finally, Bob Anderson emerged from the plane and gave me the dirtiest look of all.

Catching up with Newhart, I said, "Bob, why is everyone so pissed off?"

He replied, "Pierre, the next time you charter a plane, be sure the asshole pilot doesn't come back and start talking show business to your passengers. We couldn't get rid of the son of a bitch."

I said, "Newhart, he's the chairman of the board of Rockwell

International. They make the Saberliner you flew in on, not to mention spacecraft."

"Well, who knew?" said Newhart.

Bob Anderson came to me and said, "Pierre, that's the last time I'll fly asshole actors anywhere. I kept going back to talk to them and they were rude as hell to me." I'd forgotten to tell them who their pilot was. A simple omission, but, in this case, a serious one. Would I be a good travel agent? I don't think so.

Another Newhart story involves my son Johnny. While in San Diego, Johnny was involved in a terrible accident, and we thought we were going to lose him. He was put in intensive care. It was absolutely devastating. Not long after we'd been assured that Johnny was going to be okay, I received a big box from Bob Newhart. Now, I have a reputation for being the kind of guy who spills food all over himself. Whenever I see people who know me, they automatically look to see if I have a stain on my shirt. Anyway, I thought it was sweet of Bob to think of me at a time like this. That really is what friends are for. In the box was a surgical gown stained with ketchup, gravy, and mustard. There was also a note from Bob saying, "I just wanted to make sure Johnny recognizes you when he comes around." I thought that was hilarious.

I love Diana Ross. Yet two of my biggest disappointments and embarrassments in show business had to do with that wonderful lady. To begin with, in 1976, I was producing my sixth Grammy Awards telecast at the Hollywood Palladium. James Mahoney, one of Hollywood's top publicists, came to me and said, "Pierre, you put the live Grammy Awards together, you put up your own money, and you produce the show year after year. But nobody knows it. The producer of the Oscars show is all over the press, and so is the producer of the Emmys, and they're hired hands. You are the entrepreneur. You're the one who guarantees the money to make the Grammys happen. You should be out there, and people should know about it."

Mahoney handled all the big stars—Frank Sinatra, for one—so I listened carefully to what he had to say. Then I said, "Okay, maybe you're right. What should I do?"

"Listen to me."

"Okay," I said. I hired him.

Then he sat down with me and laid out the plan: "The day before the Grammy Awards, every big recording star and all the presidents of the record companies are in town."

"So?" I said.

"So you should put on a tremendous spread—champagne and caviar, great food. Get Chasen's to cater and invite the bigwigs for lunch right there at the Palladium. Seat them in the lobby, where they can see the lights and the sets going up and get the feel of being behind the scenes. Most of all, let them know that this is Pierre Cossette's show. We'll display a big photograph of you and a sign that says, 'Pierre Cossette Productions Welcomes You to the Sixth Annual Grammy Awards.' We'll put it up right in the middle of the buffet."

"But the buffet will cost a fortune," I insisted.

"So what?" answered Mahoney. "It will put you and your company on the map for all time. I'll personally see to it that all the top press people are there."

Well, the big day arrived. The Palladium lobby looked magnificent. Chasen's had done a terrific job—Dom Perignon champagne, chilled lobster, crab, shrimp, and all the trimmings. At 12:30 p.m., I went to the parking lot entrance to wait for the limousines. I wanted to personally escort as many of my guests as I could into the luncheon. I was following Jim Mahoney's orders to the letter.

The first to arrive was Diana Ross. I opened the limo door for her and proudly escorted her into the Palladium. It was quite a long walk, so we had a chance to chat. She said that she thought what I was doing was great for the recording industry. As we entered the lobby, I stopped dead in my tracks. I felt faint. I became catatonic. Here was the spectacle before me: a crew of 150 stagehands munching on caviar, hors d'oeuvres, and lobster and guzzling champagne. Hard-hats rushed over to me saying, "This is the greatest production company we've ever worked for," and catered meals from other production companies "never come close to this."

By the time all of my invited guests had arrived, all that remained of the fabulous buffet were empty serving dishes and hundreds of dirty napkins. To make things worse, Jim Mahoney showed up and blasted me for being stupid enough to allow something like that to happen. And it was my fault, in fact: I had neglected to announce to the crew that their lunch would not be catered that day.

The next night, just before airtime, Mahoney said to me, "Look, we've got to make up for that fiasco yesterday."

"How?"

"Well, you've got to go to the press tent at least once during the show. I'll find you the best spot, where the press and television people will be sure to recognize you as the major domo."

When the stars appearing in our show leave the stage, they report immediately to the press tent for still photographs; then the television crews shoot them; finally, they do interviews. Halfway through the show, Mahoney came into the booth and said, "Come with me." Bette Midler and Cher had just taken their bows and were heading for the press tent. We headed over there too. The second we arrived, Mahoney grabbed me and shoved me between Bette and Cher, but I knew both ladies rather well, so it didn't bother me. Suddenly, an army of three hundred press photographers was snapping away, and I was momentarily blinded by the flashes.

For a brief moment, I felt like a star myself. But the illusion was quickly destroyed when someone shouted from the back of the room, "Who's the fat guy in the middle?" I've produced the Grammys umpteen times since then, but I never again set foot in the press tent.

Foopie used to say to me, "Pierre, the publicity will come. When you force it, it's bullshit. You'll get it when you deserve to get it." That was good advice, and since that fiasco I have taken it to heart.

I did have another embarrassing moment connected with Diana Ross, but it occurred much later—in 1993. I had gotten to know her pretty well by then, largely because I'd been renting space in my building to her production company for some time. On the occasion of the 1993 Grammy Awards, the Recording Academy was presenting a Living Legend tribute to Diana Ross, an honor that had previously gone to Paul McCartney, Bob Dylan, and Barbra Streisand. We were planning to develop an eight-minute spot for the tribute that would include video segments, stills, and film clips—a montage of her great career.

Diana, her production assistant, and I met for lunch at 21 to work out the details. We found that we were in agreement about how it should be handled, and the lunch ended on a very positive note. A week later, I called Mike Greene, president of the Recording Academy, and I told him how enthusiastic Diana and I were about the spot.

"What about guest stars?" said Mike.

"We didn't discuss that," I said, quickly adding, "but it won't be a problem."

"Well, I made a deal with Darryl Busby, the president of Motown, that we'd only air the presentation of the award if Diana could deliver Michael Jackson," said Mike.

"You didn't tell me that," I said, trying to keep my cool.

"I thought I did," replied Mike. "But it's no problem—Darryl said they'd work it out."

They never did work it out, and Diana Ross finally had to be told that the segment wouldn't be aired. There was absolutely nothing I could do to save it, and I felt miserable about it. Diana didn't understand what had gone wrong, and I know that she was terribly disappointed. She wrote me a beautiful letter, which I never answered. I had every intention of doing so, but I simply didn't. One day, somehow, I'm going to make it up to her. Diana Ross is an extraordinary talent, and she should be put on a pedestal for her contribution to the industry; she is one of the principal reasons that the record business has grown from a billion-dollar industry to a thirty-one-billion-dollar one.

Advertisers play a big part in television, and if you want to be a successful producer, you must learn to treat them right. Here's an example. My friend Jerry Perenchio was promoting a heavyweight title fight between George Foreman and Joe Frazier, to be held in the Nassau County Coliseum in Long Island. Jerry gave me two fabulous tickets—third row ringside—and I invited Sandy Reisenbach to join me. Sandy was head man at Grey Advertising. Grey was, and is, a huge agency, and I was doing lots of business with them, so I thought that this would be a perfect way to "service the account."

I hired a limo, picked Sandy up, and off we went. Once we were settled in our seats, Sandy suddenly said, "Oh my God!" and pointed to the seat in front of him. In a loud whisper, he said, "That's Liz Taylor! I've idolized her my entire life. I've seen every picture she's ever made, over and over." Since I was in the business, spotting Liz Taylor didn't mean a lot to me, but Sandy Reisenbach went bananas. He was so engrossed with the back of her head that I don't know how much he saw of the fight. Afterwards, as we stood in line waiting for our limo, a commotion started behind us. It was like Beatlemania revisited. The person being pushed and mauled was Liz Taylor. Everybody wanted an autograph. She was with Cliff Perlman, owner of Caesar's Palace. Cliff was doing all he could to control the masses, but he still had to stay there and wait for his limo.

My limo arrived first, and before I knew what I was doing, I yelled out, "Cliff, you take my limo, and I'll wait for yours." Extremely grateful, Liz climbed in and motioned to Sandy to come and sit next to her. She was probably thinking that it was his limo, so he was entitled to ride in it. I turned to Sandy and said, "No, you're coming with me." Then I watched his expression go from bright sunshine to dark rain clouds. Liz said, "See you back in town, then," and the limo pulled away.

Sandy was so pissed off that he wouldn't even speak to me. But he managed to control his temper until an hour later, when we were still waiting for Perlman's limousine. We saw some limos parked a few hundred yards away, so we walked over and asked each driver if his was the Cliff Perlman limo. At last we found one who said, "Yo, what about it?" I explained to him that Mr. Perlman had taken my limo, and I was supposed to take his.

"Bullshit, pal," he said. "Mr. Perlman is downstairs at Mr. Perenchio's fight party."

"There is no after-fight party," I told him.

"Yeah, then what's Mr. Perlman doing down there?"

"He's not down there," I insisted, "he's in town with Liz Taylor in my limousine."

"Fuck off," the driver said, turning away.

It was now 1:00 a.m. Only three humans were left outside the Nassau County Coliseum: Sandy, the limo driver, and me. Finally, the driver caved in to my pressure and said, "Okay, I'll take youse bums to Manhattan for one hundred bucks!" I paid it.

It was a long time before I sold another show to Grey Advertising. But that wasn't the end of the story. Four weeks later, I got a $2,700 bill from the limo service. Liz Taylor had used my limo for the next ten days, assuming that Cliff Perlman was paying the bill. I agonized about what to do. I finally paid the bill, remembering the many times that Perlman had picked up my hotel and dinner tabs at Caesar's Palace in Las Vegas.

A couple of months later, when I figured that Sandy had calmed down, I wrote to tell him about the limo bill. He sent back a note saying that he'd "always believed in happy endings." Now, every time I see him, I say, "Liz told me to say hello." It brings a smile.

By now, you've probably figured out that in showbiz, selling your product can be tough. Let me tell you about Art Fisher. Art was a terrific television director. He'd won several Emmys by the time he was thirty-four, and he had a very bright future. It was 1979, and Art was selling me an idea for a weekly television series, asking me to put up the money for the pilot. I was very reluctant to do it, but he just kept after me (as I would have done in his position). I was still refusing him the day I heard a tremendous boom that made my whole office building shake. I looked out my tenth-floor window, and there was Art Fisher, at the controls of a helicopter he'd just purchased. In the passenger seat was a guy flipping cue cards, each containing a pitch for Art's show.

Art was as renowned for his derring-do as he was for his creativity, so it didn't surprise me to see him combining his talents— flying a helicopter while pitching an idea. A few weeks later, however, Art was killed in his helicopter. He'd been up to more dangerous tricks, and it did him in.

One year, Kenny Rogers hosted the Grammy Awards. (Kenny and I have been friends since he was the bass player for the Kirby Stone Four; I'd booked the band at the Mapes Hotel back in 1954.) Kenny's voice had been failing all week, and he was worried about it. Sure enough, just before show time, it gave out on him. Ten minutes before he was to go live in front of one hundred million viewers worldwide, his manager, Ken Kragen, was telling me, "Kenny can't go on." I rushed to Kenny's dressing room. Kenny held up a note that said, "I'm sorry."

Talk about panic. I ran out and scanned the audience. There was Dionne Warwick. I had produced a special for her at CBS, so I knew how she worked. I raced down to her and said, "Dionne, we go on in six minutes, and Kenny Rogers's voice is gone. Will you host the show?" Dumbfounded, Dionne stared at me in silence. "Look, Dionne," I said, "you're a pro. You have the credentials, and everything you have to say is up on cue cards. If changes need to be made, we'll make them while the show is in progress."

Her eyes opened wide, but she said yes. We ran backstage, arriving there two minutes before the start time. While I explained to Dionne where she had to position herself on the stage, word that she was replacing Kenny was traveling like lightning. With one minute to go, we looked up to see Kenny Rogers and Ken Kragen standing there. Kragen said, "Pierre, Kenny's going to give it a try. If he can't make it, he'll call Dionne in from the wings."

Not only did Kenny finish the entire three-hour show, but also his voice got better as he went along. It wasn't the first time I'd seen an entertainer or athlete summon up all of his or her strength and spirit and play through an injury.

It's often mishaps such as that one that result in the best stories. I remember doing a live show from the Convention Center in Miami, when, five minutes before show time, the dance captain told me that the dancers were refusing to go on because the floor was too slippery. Since the dancers opened the show, I went crazy. I grabbed the stage manager and told him about the problem. "I'll fix it in three minutes," he assured me. He and his crew sprayed industrial-strength stickum on the floor; the dance captain tried it out and indicated that it was okay. A minute later, the dancers went on and danced their hearts out, moving free as the wind.

Emcee Jackie Gleason then announced our first guest star: Bob Newhart. Well, the director had forgotten to tell Bob that because of the stickum he had to take a different route to the stage from the one he had rehearsed. So as he walked out, wearing rubber-soled shoes, his feet stuck to the floor. With each step he took, he was forced to wrench his foot off the floor. Finally, he made it to the microphone. The audience, of course, thought he was doing a comedy bit; backstage, the stagehands, the dancers, and I cracked up. Newhart tells this story often to illustrate the perils of working for Pierre Cossette Productions.

By 1981, my business was in high gear. Foopie and I were thoroughly enjoying our success. Johnny was twenty-four and out of college, running an off-Broadway theater in New York. Andy was seventeen and working towards a career in music.

It became clear that I needed more working space. I had always rented offices, but the time had come for me to buy a building. The ICM building in Beverly Hills—eleven stories and 105,000 square feet—was up for sale. ICM, the second largest entertainment agency in town, was the principal occupant. It was far more building than I wanted or needed. However, when I saw that MCA Distributing Corporation had ten thousand square feet on the first floor, I was sold.

With Bette Davis

With Bruce Springsteen

With Peter Falk

On the set of the NBC Christmas Special in Rovaniemi, Finland

The Cossettes with Céline Dion and René Angelil

With Kathie Lee Gifford

With Sean Connery

RON WOLFSON

With Bono

With Lauryn Hill

With former New York City mayor Rudy Giuliani

With Ethel Kennedy and Frank Gifford

The Cossettes with George and Barbara Bush

With Sheryl Crow

With B.B. King and Eric Clapton

With Ricky Martin

The Cossettes with Debbie and Andy Williams

With (from left to right) DJ Jazzy Jeff, Will Smith, and Chris Rock

Pierre and Mary, 'Mother of Five'

After I bought the building, I couldn't wait to call Lew Wasserman. I said, "Lew, I bought the ICM building, and I expect you to keep your space nice and clean." Lew laughed. I was flattered that Lew hadn't wanted me to leave MCA back in those early days, and I'm sure he was pleased that one of his boys had made it on his own and hadn't become one of those guys walking around outside trying to get back in.

Foopie and I had started out together on the very bottom rung of the show business ladder. I was barely scraping by on my two-hundred-dollars-a-week job at MCA. Things began to look up when Foopie became Harry Cohn's private secretary at $150 a week. Slowly, we had saved enough money to buy a home in Brentwood, but we still had to keep our fingers crossed that we'd be able to make our mortgage payments.

Twenty-nine years later, a TV special I was producing for HBO took us to London, England. Following the show, which had taken place at the Wembley Arena, I decided to surprise Foopie. I hired a Rolls Royce and a chauffeur to pick us up at the Connaught Hotel, where we were staying. We took the Rolls to France aboard a hovercraft and drove on to the Plaza Athénée Hotel in Paris. Foopie was thrilled. It was a truly romantic vacation, the kind of thing we'd never done before. Foopie's left leg started hurting her during our last couple of days in France, and we had to curtail our walking. We returned home on the Concorde. Foopie kept telling me how impressed she was that after almost thirty years of marriage I was putting this heavy hit on her. It made me feel good too. She deserved it. We both deserved it.

At home, Foopie's leg kept hurting. I told her that a charley horse was the oldest complaint known to medicine and she should have a doctor look at it. She did. Three days later, the doctor called and told me that my wife had a malignant tumor in her leg that had to be operated on immediately. I took her to the hospital for presurgical X rays. Again, we received a call from the doctor; this time, we were asked to come to his office. He talked us through the X rays, showing us how the cancer had started in Foopie's lung and traveled down into her leg.

Six weeks later, the day after our thirtieth anniversary, Foopie died. During those last six weeks, she underwent chemotherapy and lost her hair. I brought her three dozen different wigs from the wardrobe department. Weak as she was, she thought the wigs were hilarious, and we laughed as she tried them on, one after another. That was our last laugh together. When I left her that day, I pulled the car to the side of the road and screamed at the top of my voice, "I don't want Foopie to die!" I could write a book about Foopie's last weeks, but even now it would be too painful.

For months after Foopie's death, I lived in a daze. I was totally lost. Whenever I'm really troubled about something, I head for the sea. It's my church. So, naturally, when Foopie died I walked the beach a lot. I used to sing that great song "The Summer Wind," which Frank Sinatra had turned into such a big hit. I'd sing it over and over, choking up at the line, "And softer than a piperman one day it came for you / And I lost you to the summer wind / The summer wind has come and gone, but those lonely nights go on and on."

As I was starting to come out of this state, I accepted an invitation to Aaron Spelling's birthday party, which was being held at Chasen's. I called Angie Dickinson to ask if she'd be my first date. She wasn't in, so I left a message, but Angie didn't return my call. I phoned back a few days later, and her maid asked me if the call was personal or professional. I said that it was personal, explaining that I wanted to invite Angie to Aaron Spelling's party. The maid said,

"Oh, that's delightful! I'm sure she'd love to. I'll see her when she comes home this evening, and I'll let you know tomorrow." The maid did not call back. I looked in the mirror and saw a face that was not Tom Selleck's. It was my own, and I was one defeated puppy.

Later, at a banquet in my honor, Angie got up and told the story, adding that the maid had never given her the message because she was hoping that if I didn't hear back from Angie I might invite her instead. Then Angie paused and added, "By the way, Pierre. My maid is here tonight, and I'd really like you to meet her." From the wings came a girl so beautiful that she'd put Bo Derek to shame. Some maid! It got a big laugh. Then Tommy Lasorda told of a quick trip he had made to heaven, where he saw a man with the ugliest female he'd ever seen. Tommy asked God why this man was in heaven with such an ugly woman. God explained that the man had been bad on Earth, and this was his penance. A little while later, Tommy continued, he saw Pierre, and Bo Derek was all over him. Startled, Tommy asked the Lord if Pierre had really been that good. God said, "No—Bo Derek was really bad." Another big laugh.

After the Angie Dickinson fiasco, I dated a starlet here and an actress there, all of whom were young enough to be my daughter. I had to keep coming up with all kinds of bullshit to amuse these girls. And it was all because of my friend Walter Miller, the talented producer and director who had divorced his wife at about the time Foopie had passed away. We were the same age, we were both successful and influential, and we had money to throw around. Walter had just bought a convertible Porsche, and he stored tennis rackets, air tanks, golf clubs, and everything Adidas made in his trunk. He took up with one young girl after another. It worked for him; he had a ball. But it did not work for me. I felt guilty telling the girls I dated what they wanted to hear—which was basically that I was well connected and could help them.

Well, at about this time I was producing the Grammy Awards

show in New York. Since I had no offices in New York, I made a deal with Ed Sullivan Productions to rent their offices and employ their staff for six weeks. One member of the Sullivan staff was a beautiful young girl with a great body and a personality to match. She couldn't have been more than twenty-two. She seemed to take a tremendous liking to me. I was still in the dumps, and I hadn't dated for some time.

One day, in a very flirtatious way, she came up to me and said, "What are you doing tomorrow night?"

I said, "Nothing. Why?"

"Well," she said, "there's no one here after 7:00 p.m., and I have a key to Ed Sullivan's office. It's got a bar and a new surround-sound system. We could spend a little time together, if you like."

The offices were located on the forty-sixth floor of a skyscraper on 47th Street at Fifth Avenue. The view was spectacular, especially at night. I quickly agreed to meet her. Back in my hotel room, I showered, squirted on every kind of cologne I could find, and stood in front of the mirror examining my face and body. Soon I was seeing Robert Redford, Sean Connery, and even a hint of Tom Cruise. I could almost feel the hair growing on my chest. Clearly, I still had it—I was ready!

The next night at 8:15, I was standing next to the girl, looking out the window at the Big Apple sparkling below us. We had had a martini. She was hitting on me. I thought I had died and gone to heaven. She took me by the hand and said, "Let's go over and sit on the sofa." What had been pudgy for some time now became very hard. She pulled me down onto the sofa and said, "Can you spend this weekend with me on Long Island?" I exhaled a strong "yesss"— much the way a snake hisses. She then reached for her purse, opened it, and said, "There's something I want to show you." I said to myself, "My God, she brought her own condom!" But out of her purse came half a dozen pictures of a very attractive middle-aged lady.

I had no idea what was going on. As I thumbed through the photos, the girl gushed, "I'm so glad you're coming to Long Island. You're so perfect for Mom!" In that instant, everything collapsed. First, the hopeful little thing between my legs, then all of the macho behavior I had reserved for such rare moments. I still dream of what might have been.

At the 1982 Grammy Awards, Steve Martin and I were talking in my little cubbyhole, stage left. Steve was to present the award for Best Comedy Album. He said to me, "Tell me when it's exactly one minute before I'm to go on." The time came, and I told him. He immediately proceeded to take his pants off, and before I could holler, "What the hell are you doing?" Martin was headed for center stage in his tuxedo jacket, black tie, and red-and-white undershorts.

From stage right came a dry-cleaning delivery guy carrying a pair of pants. He quickly walked over to Steve and said, "Sorry I'm a little late." Steve put on the pants while he was presenting the award. The reason it worked so well is that no one—not me, not the director, not anyone—knew about it beforehand.

I once had dinner in Ojai with Steve, who has a beautiful home nearby. The dinner was my treat, and, because I know that he's a wine connoisseur, I invited Steve to order the wine. I thought his selection was pretty good—not great, but pretty good. That my knowledge of wine is limited became apparent when the check came and I saw that the charge for one bottle of wine was six hundred dollars. Steve must have noticed that the color of my face changed, because he laughed and said, "I love to do that to producers, but only those who can afford it." Some compliment!

Mother of Five

TO MY GOOD FORTUNE, I met Mary Ufland. She was mature and beautiful, and I liked her so much that I was able to brush aside the fact that she had five children, ranging in age from six to seventeen. I didn't have to bullshit Mary, and that was one of the many reasons I found her so attractive. I soon nicknamed her "Mary, The Mother of Five," which I later shortened to just plain "Five."

Born Mary Daly, Five was adopted as an infant by a wealthy and successful couple. Her father, Ralph Blum, partnered with Charlie Feldman to found the Famous Artists talent agency, and her mother was Carmel Myers, a movie star of the twenties, thirties, and forties and a TV personality of the early fifties. The couple brought Mary from an Augusta, Georgia, orphanage to Beverly Hills, where they lived in a mansion across the street from the Beverly Hills Hotel. She attended all the right schools: the Brearley School in New York, Shipley in Bryn Mawr, Pennsylvania, Bennett College in Millbrook, New York, and Columbia University.

My attorney, Dick Harris, who's been with me for decades and absolutely loves Five, didn't even want to meet her at first. "You're out of your mind thinking of marrying a woman with five kids," he said, for openers. And my friend Walter Miller was beside himself: "How can you do that? You've already got two kids. John's on his own and Andy's twenty. You're almost home free. And you're blowing a great bachelor life! Look at me—I have a different girl every night. I take them home, they cook for me, I fuck 'em, they're gone in the morning, and I start again. Never a dull moment."

I listened carefully to my friends, and then I married the Mother of Five. On our first date, I took her to see Jerry Lee Lewis at the Palomino in the Valley. Our next date was a drive to the California State Fair in Pomona. I thought her two younger kids—Jossie, seven, and Jennifer, twelve—would like the fair, so we brought them along. There, we entered a huge building that looked like an airplane hangar. Inside were thousands of chickens, roosters, and turkeys— literally thousands. Five turned to me and joked, "I haven't seen this many cocks since I was in college!" How can you not love a girl like that?

The first time I tried to tell Mary Ufland how much I liked her, I said, with deep sincerity, "You know, to me you feel like an old shoe." Well, I know she understood me, but for weeks she referred to herself as "the old shoe." I've never been one for flowery romantic talk. What can I say?

When I met her, Mary was running five miles a day (now she runs marathons). In other words, she was in great physical condition—not something you could have said about me. In fact, I had been having a problem with my feet, and the doctor had told me to get walking. Mary got me walking and swimming.

In our early dating days, we had a hard time having a close relationship because Mary lived with her kids on Point Dume in Malibu, and I was living alone in L.A. It just wouldn't have worked for us to move in together at that point. But one day it occurred to me to invite her to come with me on a business trip I had to take to New York. "Then we can fly up to Montreal on the weekend," I said. "I can show you where I was born, and you can meet my relatives." Well, Mary did come with me, and she fell in love with my relatives instantly. Most of the menfolk, like me, have little bellies and little dimples. Two of my cousins now have flocks of kids. Mary and I both take real joy in visiting the Cossette homestead. But I'm getting ahead of myself.

After we had returned from another stolen holiday—this time a fabulous three weeks in Europe—the Mother of Five and I were walking on the beach one day, holding hands and talking. I heard myself saying, "When we get married, we should . . ." Five said, "What do you mean, 'when' we get married? You mean 'if' we get married." So I said, "I don't know. Would you like to get married?" We started to get excited by the idea and to think more seriously about what it would mean to her five kids and my two. Fortunately, my kids were crazy about Mary.

Soon after that spontaneous proposal, Five and I were having dinner with Jerry Perenchio and his fiancée, Marge. We told them of our plan (no longer just an idea). We wanted to be married at Our Lady of Malibu, a small Catholic church. Jerry asked us how many people we were going to invite. We had settled on fifty or sixty after toying with the idea of five or six hundred. Then Jerry suggested that we tie the knot at their home in Malibu. Five and I looked at each other, and in one voice said, "That would be great! Thank you so much."

This is how the most opulent wedding in the history of Hollywood came about. If you think I'm exaggerating, here's what Hollywood's principal PR firm, Rogers and Cowan, called it: "the greatest wedding in the history of Hollywood." And I have it all on film. Jerry Perenchio put on an extravaganza for us. Jerry, one of the wealthiest individuals in show business—owner of the largest estate in Bel Air, a mansion in Malibu, a fleet of jets, and one of the most beautiful apartments in New York City—provided us with the perfect setting: his golf course. Jerry had constructed a twelve-acre golf course in the "backyard" of his Malibu property, completely enclosed by a stone wall.

As our plans advanced, the guest list swelled from 50 to 520. The ceremony itself was to be held in a wedding tent, where guests would be greeted by a chorus of eighty gospel singers, the men in white tuxedos and the women in white gowns. The chorus would be surrounded by seven white concert grand pianos.

On the big day, the ceremony moved along without a hitch until the judge said some words about promising to be faithful. In that solemn moment, I blurted out: "Wait a minute! I want to negotiate that point." It got a big laugh, even from the Mother of Five. The ceremony ended, and everyone left the tent and headed for an enormous carnival area. There, guests had their pick of amusements and attractions: bumper cars, a huge Ferris wheel, prizes galore—much better than what you'd find at a state fair.

After they'd spent an hour on the circus midway, the guests were guided into a huge circus tent to drink Dom Perignon and nibble on caviar, lobster, and other delicacies; then came a sumptuous dinner, catered by Chasen's. All the while, Les Brown and His Band of Renown and the rock band Billy and the Beaters played on. Following the dinner was a three-ring circus every bit as fantastic as what you'd see at Madison Square Garden. There were trapeze acts, elephant acts, daredevil acts, trained horses—the works. The final act was a team of four white ponies pulling a cart containing a ten-foot-high wedding cake. Jerry came into the center ring, stood in front of the cake (which was four feet taller than he was), and toasted the bride and groom. I stood up and said, "I can't believe that someone would do this for us. This is absolutely unbelievable. On the other hand, when I think about it, what are friends for?" That got a big laugh too.

A year later, Jerry and Marge were married. I gave the stag dinner for Jerry at Chasen's and invited the who's who of Hollywood. Naturally, I put on a show. It included a singing group that I'd put together featuring Jerry's son, John. At the end of the show, I got up and announced that party girls were about to descend. Then I added, "They'll probably sit on your laps, but we have to honor the new sexual harassment laws, and that means don't touch them." That said, I shouted, "Bring in the broads!" and the band started playing classic stripper music.

Beforehand, we'd called each of the guests' wives and asked them if they wanted to get in on the fun. Marge and Five took them off to Western Costume to select the hooker outfit of their choice. For the day of the stag party, I hired four buses to pick up the wives at a designated location. They were due to arrive at Chasen's just before their grand entrance.

Believe it or not, it took the guys quite a few minutes to realize what was going on. Marge sang a supersexy version of "My Heart Belongs to Daddy." What a night! It gave me great pleasure to see Jerry having such a good time; it was wonderful to be able to do something for him in return for the fabulous wedding party he had given us.

The day after Five and I married, I came to the sudden understanding that I was now stepfather to five children. Sure, I knew that in marrying Five I was taking on her children too, but I hadn't realized that I wasn't really prepared for it. Jossie was eight, Jennifer was starting high school, Chris was in high school, Ann had just finished, and John, the old man of twenty-four, was an agent at

Creative Arts Agency. Of course, there was a period of adjustment. We all just stared at each other for a while. Somehow, everyone ended up approving of everyone else, and I found myself once again advising an eight year old and a twelve year old on what to do with their young lives. I called myself "Superstep."

Five and the two younger girls had moved into my place on the beach in Malibu. The thing that bothered me most in those early days was the fact that the toilet seat was always down. Before long, we bought a larger house, still on the beach (which had been owned by financial icon Norton Simon), and we lived there for many years. Jennifer now lives in Colorado, where Five owns a house, and Andy rents a home that I bought in Arizona. Most of the traveling we do these days is from one of our houses to another—Beverly Hills, New York, Canada, Palm Springs. I even bought a farm near Claremont, Oklahoma.

After Five and I had been married for a couple of years, my old friend Walter Miller started inviting me to have dinner with him on a regular basis. Finally I said, "Walter, what happened to all those girls you take home every night? Can't you have dinner with them?"

Walter answered, "Yes, but sometimes I get lonely and I need someone to talk to."

I said, "Look Walter, I'm not going to have dinner with you. I'm going home to Malibu to be with Mary. That's my comfort zone. That's where I want to be. And I'll tell you one more thing, Walter. Since I've been married to Mary, I've not had one strange piece of ass."

Walter looked at me and said, "That Mary looks like a strange piece of ass to me."

When I told Five this story, she called all of her girlfriends and told them. She got a great laugh out of it. I've now been married to the Mother of Five for almost twenty years, and what I told Walter still holds true. Still, as happy as I am with Mary, there hasn't been one day that I haven't thought of Foopie. Mary understands this, and I know that Foopie would have loved her.

In 1984, the Multiple Sclerosis Foundation, in appreciation for the many fundraising benefits I had done for them, decided to hold a dinner at the Beverly Hilton Hotel in my honor. It was to be a high-priced affair for 1,220 guests. I was reluctant to accept the honor. Most of these tributes are for major celebrities who can bring in the paying guests without much difficulty. My nightmare was that with Pierre Cossette as the draw, we'd be lucky to sell two hundred tickets. Worse yet, we could sell six hundred and have a half-empty room. But the truth is that I'd made a lot of friends along the way, and, thank God, it saved the occasion for me: we were filled to capacity.

On the dais were the presidents of Twentieth Century Fox, Paramount, Universal, MGM, Warner Brothers, NBC, ABC, and CBS, plus Peter Ueberroth, Tommy Lasorda, and Ann-Margret. For the show itself, I had Jack Lemmon, Andy Williams, Peter Falk, Angie Dickinson, Bob Newhart, Frank Gifford, Steve Allen, and Jerry Lee Lewis. That lineup ensured that every ticket sold, and sold quickly. I went to work making calls, starting with Peter Falk. He agreed to do the show, but he said, "You know I don't dance, or sing, or do standup. So what will you have me do?"

Quick thinker that I had become, I laid it out for him. Halfway through the show, as Andy Williams was singing his heart out on "Moon River," Detective Columbo would walk on wearing his trademark rumpled trench coat. Apologizing for the intrusion, he'd say, in his characteristic drawl, "I'm Detective Columbo. The chief sent me down here to find out why you're giving a tribute dinner for . . ." (he'd pause, rummaging through his pockets for a piece of paper with the name written on it) ". . . Pierre Cossette. Well, see, the chief never heard of him—no one else in the department knows this guy either, so I'm here to investigate. I'm really sorry to bother you."

Columbo would then turn to the audience and remark, "Wow. This is a fancy party. Look at all those tuxedos and long gowns. Lady, those earrings are really something." Turning back to an appropriately shocked Andy Williams, he'd continue: "Anyway, I looked into this for the chief and found out this guy, Pierre Cossette, is some kind of producer. So, the chief wanted to know what he's produced. So, I gave him a list—I've got it right here—of shows this Pierre Cossette has produced."

I explained to Peter that I would give him a list of every turkey or bomb I'd ever been involved in. And, believe me, producers have a lot of them. Peter liked it. At the dinner, the bit played perfectly. The audience roared. I consider it one of the most memorable theatrical moments of my life.

Ethel Kennedy is a very good friend of mine, and I love her dearly. I met the Kennedys through Andy Williams. He invited me to come along once when he was scheduled to do a show for them in Washington, D.C. I was pretty excited at the prospect. Ethel herself was supposed to pick us up at the airport. We were waiting for her when a beat-up old station wagon pulled up. The driver, a lady, was shouting, "Andy! Andy!" That was my introduction to Ethel Kennedy.

If I've ever had fun with somebody, it's Ethel Kennedy. I stayed at Hyannisport a few times. On one occasion, I took my son Andy along. He was seventeen. To this day, he remembers an hour he spent on the beach with Jacqueline Onassis. On one of my visits, Ethel invited me aboard her prized boat *The Resolute*. As I soon discovered, even a stuntman would be leery of going to sea with Ethel Kennedy. She'd challenge *The Queen Mary* to get out of her way. Packing too much food and rounding up too many people, she'd say, "Come on, let's go everybody!"

Once, she said, "Come on, we're going up into the high rapids where there's rafting." I had never been rafting before, but I seldom turn down the chance for adventure. At some point along the way, I was thrown into the raging waters (that's the way they looked to me, anyway). I bobbed there thinking I had reached the end of my life. The rapids dragged me about six hundred yards before a couple of Kennedy kids managed to pull me back into the boat. Ethel looked at me with a big smile and said, "Well, Pierre, wasn't that fun?"

A few years ago, Ethel came to Beverly Hills as the guest of Carrol Rosenbloom, the owner of the L.A. Rams. She asked me to be her escort to a political affair, and I picked her up in my new, fully equipped Chevrolet Blazer—not exactly a limousine, but she liked it. After the dinner and the speeches, I took Ethel back to Rosenbloom's house. We stood at the door as she rang the bell. No answer. She rang again. Still no answer. She couldn't figure it out, and neither could I. Then I had an idea. I explained it to Ethel, and she was game. We went back to the Blazer, and I pulled it to within twenty feet of the mansion's front door. Together, we slowly let out the winch until it reached the door. Then we carefully attached it to the two large door handles. We got back into the truck and started laughing, fantasizing about what might happen if we went ahead with the plan.

For over an hour, we sat there trying to decide whether we should do it, agonizing over the decision. We were both very friendly with Carrol, and we thought Carrol would get a laugh out of it. And how much could it cost to fix the door after we popped it off?

Finally, we walked down to the Bel Air sheriff's substation, which was nearby, and called the house. Carrol was a little pissed off to get a phone call at 2:00 a.m. We explained to him that Ethel had no key to the house and said we'd be there in five minutes. He couldn't open the door for us because it was tied to the winch, so he walked around from the side entrance. Taking one look at our setup, Carrol roared with laughter. "Why didn't you do it?" he said.

To this day, every time I see Ethel Kennedy we recall that night and accuse each other of chickening out.

Irving "Swifty" Lazar, who died in 1994, was a famous name in Hollywood circles. Even outside of Hollywood, Swifty was noted for the fabulous parties he gave every year following the Academy Awards telecast. Much to the chagrin of the academy, which always held its own party, all the stars would head for Swifty's.

In 1984, Swifty called me from Europe and said, "Pierre, I can't make it back for my Oscar party. I'd like you to host it."

Taken aback, I said, "Swifty, I don't have that kind of clout in the motion picture end of the business."

"You don't need it," he said. "I will personally invite everyone. All you have to do is greet people. Smile your big smile and table-hop."

So I said yes.

Swifty knew how successful I'd been at filling Chasen's with showbiz heavyweights for my annual Super Bowl Party. Still, I was surprised and honored, because if I had one showbiz idol, it was Swifty Lazar. From the time I started out at MCA, it had never been my ambition to become Lew Wasserman, Michael Eisner, Mike Ovitz, Barry Diller, David Geffen, or any other corporate leader in the entertainment industry. I wanted to become Swifty Lazar.

Swifty was a loner, a one-man show. He didn't have to check with anyone for anything. Except during his early days at MCA, he was always his own boss. He maintained the respect of the industry with a desk, a secretary, and a wastebasket. He went head-to-head with all the giant agencies and won more times than not. He was, and is, my hero.

Some years back, I had an idea for a Christmas special. I sent it to Brandon Tartikoff, then president of NBC. The idea was a simple one: we'd go to the North Pole in search of Santa Claus. The host would be Andy Williams, and the guests would be the little kids from *The Bill Cosby Show* and some other NBC shows.

"Great idea," Tartikoff said, and he bought the show. Off we went—the kids, their families, and the various technical people we needed. After several plane switches, we arrived in Rovaniemi, Finland, the closest city to the North Pole. Rovaniemi, as you can imagine, has more reindeer than people. Production came to a halt before we started, because there was no snow. No one had seen the likes of it in fifty-four years. Furthermore—obviously—there was no snow-making equipment in the entire country. We were held up for four days waiting for snow machines to arrive from London, so as the show's producer, I paid the cast and crew to do nothing.

The day after we finished the shoot, we were caught in the damnedest snowstorm the people of Rovenimi had ever seen. We were snowed in for two days. I lost a lot of money on the show; but fortunately it was a big hit, and NBC repeated it the following year. So I ended up making money on it after all.

In 1989, Andy Williams was presenting the Grammy Life Achievement Award to Bessie Smith. Sitting in the front row was Bruce Springsteen, who was at the height of his "Born in the U.S.A." period. Before the end of the show, Andy said, "Pierre, you've got to do me a favor. I want to meet Bruce Springsteen." Well, the whole world wanted to meet Bruce Springsteen, and I didn't even know him.

"Andy," I said, "How do you expect me to do this? He'll be mobbed as soon as the show is over."

Andy replied, "Look, I've done you a million favors, and now I'm asking you to do one for me. I really want to meet him."

I said, "Okay. Be in my backstage office as soon as the show ends."

Wow, this was some assignment. The only thing I had going for me was that Bruce Springsteen knew who I was and what I looked like, since, as executive producer, I always go on stage to talk to the audience just before the show starts. So, while the final credits were rolling, I made my way to where he was sitting and said, "Bruce, I can bail you out of a mob scene if you'll come back to my office and wait until the crowd dies down. I'll have your limo pick you up backstage." I was lucky. Bruce said, "That's a great idea. Thank you." And he introduced me to his mother and his fiancée.

As we headed for my office, I was feeling pretty good about this caper. I was just hoping that Springsteen wouldn't pick up on the fact that I was delivering him to Andy Williams. When I opened the door to let Bruce, his fiancée, and his mother in, I heard Bruce's mother scream, "Andy Williams! Oh my God! What a thrill, what a pleasure it is to meet you in person. You've always been my very favorite." Then Bruce said, "Andy you won't believe it, but the first song I ever sang in public was 'Moon River.' It was in high school; I made a special arrangement of it."

I was thrilled too. I even had myself believing that the whole thing was my idea. Afterwards, Andy said to me, "Hey, you know what? I'd like to meet Pavarotti." We had a good laugh.

Artists such as Bruce Springsteen, Joan Baez, Tracy Chapman, and today's rap groups are like the town criers of old who would walk through the streets yelling out the news in rhyme. Bruce's "Born in the U.S.A.," while personal to him, touched a universal sentiment. He was a town crier for the eighties, just as Baez was a town crier for the sixties. Tracy Chapman puts the bittersweet world of the ghetto into her music, and the rap groups put their messages in your face.

John Kluge is one of the richest men in the world. I knew him well enough for him to allow me to use his apartment in the Waldorf Towers in the Waldorf Astoria Hotel before I had my own place in New York. But "apartment" doesn't exactly describe the place—it had a dining room that could seat sixty.

Anyway, I was there one night, happily ensconced, wearing pajamas, when the doorbell rang. I opened the door to four policemen, guns drawn, and the hotel manager. I was scared to death. As I was standing there trying to figure out what was going on, the phone rang, and the hotel manager answered it. It was George Steinbrenner and John Kluge, calling to ask how I liked the apartment.

I took the phone. George and John were laughing so hard they were unintelligible. They had set the whole up thing by calling security to say there was a strange man in Kluge's apartment and they suspected a robbery. They let the hotel manager in on it, but not the cops. "Is this your idea of funny?" I screamed. "I could have been shot!" I went back to bed and schemed to get even with them.

The next morning, I had a breakfast date with Steinbrenner there at the Waldorf. I arrived carrying a pillowcase stuffed with neckties. George couldn't see what was in the pillowcase, but he was obviously curious. I said, "George, that was funny last night, but not really funny. I'm in show business, and I'll show you something that's really funny." I called the maitre d' over and said, "This pillowcase is filled with John Kluge's ties. He's tired of them, and he asked me to give them to you and your staff. Well, he's not really giving them away—you have to pay five dollars for each tie, but all the proceeds will go to Mr. Kluge's charity foundation."

You have to realize that the name John Kluge is pure gold at the Waldorf. The maitre d' took ten ties on the spot. George Steinbrenner was watching and listening to my spiel, absolutely dumbstruck that I had dared to steal and sell every tie John Kluge owned. Before that breakfast was over, however, he was laughing so hard that I had to pick him up off the floor. You see, comedy is leading someone down a road and then taking an outlandish turn. Sure, John Kluge was a little pissed off at first, but he finally realized that my funny response to his funny arrest was, in fact, pretty funny. I think members of the Waldorf staff are still thanking him for the tie bonanza.

The most difficult thing to do when you're producing a TV special is line up the talent. You may have an excellent concept, but you can't sell it unless you can deliver stars. I was at NBC selling a TV special to Brandon Tartikoff based on the retirement of basketball great Kareem Abdul-Jabbar, and Brandon said, "Good idea. Who are the guest stars?" I was playing golf with Peter Falk the next day, so I said, "I think Peter Falk will do it." Brandon liked this: "He's hotter than a pistol right now. That's a good start. Let me know who else."

In other words, I had a deal if I could deliver stars. The next morning, I went to work early on Peter Falk. For sixteen holes I bugged him to do my show. We were walking up the seventeenth fairway when he finally said, "Look, you can use my name, but I ain't doin' the show." I couldn't wait to call Brandon the next day to say, "I've got Peter Falk."

"Great," said Brandon. "Get three more like him and you have a deal."

Bruce Willis lived a few houses down from me in Malibu. There was no way he'd want to do this show—movie stars seldom appear on TV variety shows. But I gave him a strong pitch, and he finally started to come around.

"Who else is doing this show?" he asked.

"Peter Falk."

"Peter's doing it? Well, that makes a big difference. I'll do it."

I called Brandon and told him I had Bruce Willis. Next, I called Whoopi Goldberg. Whoopi considered herself to be overexposed on television, so she wasn't interested. But then came the magical question, "Who else is doing the show?"

"Peter Falk and Bruce Willis."

"Peter and Bruce are doing this? I'll do it."

I called Brandon and told him I had Whoopi Goldberg, Peter Falk, and Bruce Willis. He said, "You're a genius. You've got a deal." Then, because I didn't actually have Peter Falk, I pulled in James Caan using Peter, Whoopi, and Bruce as bait.

The week of the show, I saw a full-page ad in *TV Guide* that almost made me faint. Peter Falk was featured over the other stars. I hadn't counted on that. Sure enough, it wasn't long before the phone rang and my secretary said, "It's Peter Falk." Even though I knew he was going to kill me, I took the call. Peter said, "I'm looking at the *TV Guide* ad for your show." My heart was sinking. He continued, "I gotta tell you, I like the way they airbrushed my photo. I look ten years younger—you know, like a leading man."

I said nothing, waiting for the other shoe to drop. Then Peter said, "Now, I know I told you that you could use my name, and dat's okay. But I told you before and I'm telling you now: I ain't doin' the show. I ain't gonna be there." I paused for a beat, and then said, "Peter, who the fuck needs you?" I waited for his reaction. After ten beats, he started laughing. We must have laughed together for five minutes.

The show went on. It was a big success. What meant the most to me, though, is the fact that Peter Falk saved my ass. I love show business, and I love Peter Falk. I'll never forget the day Peter and I went to a football game on a bus with a bunch of actors and entertainers. Peter was in his usual garb—dirty T-shirt with a hole in it (my kind of guy); everyone else was in cashmere and chinos. When we got there, I gave an extra ticket I had to the bus driver so he could watch the game. Before we went off to find our seats, someone asked who was going to keep an eye on the bus. Peter said, "I will," and he pretended to take out his glass eye and put it on the driver's seat. Well, I had forgotten about his false eye. Oh, God, did we laugh.

Five and I have a summer home in St. Anicet, Quebec, near Valleyfield, the town where I was born. The actual house I was born in is now a restaurant known as Le Club Touriste.

Andy Williams and his wife, Debby, would occasionally come and stay with us in St. Anicet. On one of their first visits, the four of us went to dinner at Le Club Touriste, and I asked the manager to take us upstairs to the room in which I was born. There was a bed there, and on an impulse I got onto it and curled into a fetal position. Andy burst into a glorious a capella version of "Ave Maria," as he had done at Robert Kennedy's funeral. It was quite a moment for all of us.

Even funnier was the time we were all together at our house, and Andy and Debby and Five and I were looking out the living room window and talking. Suddenly, we spotted a Canadian Navy ship in the distance, coming down the St. Lawrence River. As a lark, we decided to hop into our speedboat and go out to greet it. It was a destroyer-like vessel. As we drew alongside it, the crew of maybe 350 sailors started yahooing, waving, pulling off their jackets, and twirling them in the air. Andy and I were riding in the front of the speedboat, and Andy was clearly affected by all the hoopla. "You know something," he said, "I should get out to the countryside more often. In large cities, I'm asked for my autograph, and that's about it. But look at this. These fans are hysterical."

I turned around to tell the girls what Andy had said, and what do I see but Five and Debby, bra-less, flashing their tits at the Canadian Navy—and they both have world-class tits. Andy's moment in the sun was ruined, but we've had great laughs about it ever since.

On Grammy Awards night in 1990, I was backstage with host Billy Crystal. Billy Idol was performing on stage, totally nude from the waist up. He didn't even have a chain hanging from his neck. Billy Crystal said to me, "What do you say to me stripping down to my waist when I go out to introduce the next act?"

"I love it."

"Okay, I'll do it."

So Billy took off his tuxedo jacket, vest, bow tie, and shirt; he was stripped to the waist by the time Billy Idol ended his number and was taking his applause. Billy Crystal began to move towards the podium, but I grabbed him because I'd just remembered that right after Idol we were going to commercial—a four-minute commercial break. The connection would be broken; the bit wouldn't be funny four minutes later. Billy had to put himself back together in four minutes and look impeccable when he appeared again before a hundred million people worldwide.

Later, Billy said to me, "I can't believe you forgot we were going to a commercial."

"I was excited about a great piece of comedy—I just forgot. What can I say? I blew it."

"You do remember that you asked me to host again next year?"

"Yes, I remember."

"So do I, but what if I forget?"

Billy could have crucified me for that gaff, but he didn't.

Miles Davis, a great artist and a truly wonderful human being, was also performing live that night. It was his performance trademark to turn his back to the audience and play his horn facing the band. When we were rehearsing for the show, his number ran thirty-one seconds longer than the actual recording did. Because it was to be aired live, and commercials had to be plugged in, I told him we needed his timing to be exact. "Okay, baby, let's do it again," he said. "I'll be right on time."

He did the number again, and this time it was twenty seconds too long. I said, "Miles, what are we going to do? Maybe we should play the orchestra track from your record and you can lip-synch to that."

"I don't want to do that," he said, but then he added, "I've got a perfect solution."

"What's that?" I asked.

"Well, since I'm on a separate stage, you can add a curtain. When the director wants me to finish, he can slowly drop the curtain. I'll see it and button the number."

"Great. That's fabulous," I said. "That'll work for both of us."

At show time, Miles went on, and as usual he was marvelous. Just before the end of the number, he turned his back to the audience and starting blowing his horn to the band. At precisely that moment, the curtain started to come down. Miles did not see it and continued playing. Billy Crystal was shouting, "Miles, it's over! Miles, turn around!" The TV audience didn't know what was happening, but the live audience loved it.

My proudest moment in show business came in that same year, on December 9, when I was awarded the Ellis Island Medal of Honor. This award recognizes distinguished Americans who have made significant contributions to our nation. On that day, I was sandwiched between Dan Rostenkowski, chairman of the House Ways and Means Committee, and former general Alexander Haig, but those who receive this honor come from all walks of life. Our accomplishments and contributions vary, but what we have in common is our foreign heritage.

Among those who have received this medal of honor in the past are Lee Iacocca, Henry Kissinger, Norman Schwartzkopf, Ronald Reagan, Frank Sinatra, George Steinbrenner, Lee Trevino, Barbara Walters, Bob Hope, Joe DiMaggio, Michael Eisner, Walter Cronkite, Mario Cuomo, Jacqueline Kennedy Onassis, and—of all people— Pierre Cossette from Valleyfield, Quebec. Receiving this medal on Ellis Island, with the full Marine Band playing, sent chills down my spine.

On Broadway

FOR THOSE OF YOU who don't know, there is the motion picture producer, the television producer, the record producer, the concert producer, the event producer, the rock and roll producer, and every other kind of theatrical producer you can think of. But there is no such thing as the Broadway producer. On Broadway, there is a packager, a financier, an idea man, a deal-maker, a salesman, and a money-raiser—and that's it. The title "producer" only applies to the people who raise investment dollars. I have become an expert on this subject.

Although I had been in show business since the early fifties and, by 1983, had produced almost every kind of show imaginable, I had never produced a Broadway musical. In 1989, I became convinced that the moment was right to break the British hold on the Broadway musical theater. My passion was to produce an Americana-style show that would counter all the British fare.

First, I decided that the story of Bob Wills and the Texas Playboys would make a terrific musical, and I tried every which way I could to get the rights—but I failed. Then I remembered a one-man show I had seen in 1974 at the Cort Theater on Broadway. It was the story of Will Rogers, and it starred James Whitmore. I thought James Whitmore was terrific, but I left the theater thinking that Will Rogers's story was wasted in the one-man format.

Phillip Browning, vice president of my company, had mentioned Will Rogers to me earlier, but at that point I was still gung-ho for Bob Wills. So now I called Phillip, and he made arrangements with Tim Swift for us to meet Will Rogers Junior in Bakersfield. Several meetings later, I obtained the rights to produce the life of Will Rogers as a musical—with the proviso that I would portray the true Will Rogers and not a fictionalized character.

I was new to Broadway musical production, so I played it very close to the Hollywood scene, hiring screenwriter James Lee Barrett to do the book. Barrett was a top-flight screenwriter; he had written many of John Wayne's biggest hits. He was a perfect writer for my needs, but he wanted much more money up front than the Dramatists Guild stipulated. To get him, however, I agreed to pay his asking price. Three months later, Barrett delivered an absolutely sensational script, leaving appropriate places for songs and production numbers.

I handed the script to top country composer and songwriter John Durrell, who, a few weeks later, came back to me with the songs and music we needed. My next step was to call my friend John Denver and persuade him to become a Broadway star. I sent him the book and score—and, of course, offered him the starring role. A few days later, John Denver called me, ecstatic. He definitely wanted to do it, but only if we came up with a new score. He didn't think that Durrell's music or songs were right. Obviously, Durrell was not pleased. I set up a meeting between John Durrell and John Denver in an attempt to resolve the problem, but John Denver stood firm. He liked Durrell as a songwriter, but he did not like his musical approach to Will Rogers.

Next, I called my friend Eric Sheppard. We had been agents together at MCA many years before, and he was now New York's leading Broadway theatrical agent. I said, "Eric, I'm doing something I've wanted to do all my life: a big Broadway musical. I've got the rights to the life story of Will Rogers. Not only that, I have a great script, and I have a big star—John Denver—who's committed to do it. I'm going to Federal Express it to you. Take a week to read it, and then I'll see you in New York to set up our modus operandi." A week later, I met with Eric, and he told me, "I agree that this is a terrific script, but it's written too much like a movie. You can't put it on a stage as is."

I couldn't believe what I was hearing. I immediately called James Lee Barrett and told him in no uncertain terms that he'd given me an unmakeable script. After insisting that "those Broadway people are crazy," and so on, James reluctantly admitted that he might have screwed up in his enthusiasm to write a Broadway musical. In other words, he'd gotten carried away. So, there I was, holding the rights to produce *The Will Rogers Follies* starring John Denver, forced to start from scratch with a new writer and a new composer.

Having friends in the business is everything. Eric was extremely helpful, introducing me to several potentials, and I managed to build a powerful team: Tommy Tune directed and choreographed; Peter Stone wrote the book; Cy Coleman composed the music; Betty Comden and Adolph Green wrote the lyrics; Tony Walton designed the sets; Willa Kim designed the costumes; Jules Fisher did the lighting—and on down the line. John Denver retained the starring role.

We worked on and off for the next three years. Sometimes we'd all have to fly to San Francisco, Toronto, Boston, wherever, to accommodate Tommy Tune's road schedule. We were finally closing in on the completion of the book and the score when I got a devastating phone call from John Denver. CBS had just offered him a pilot for a one-hour weekly series for the following season. It was an offer he couldn't refuse. Of course, I let him out of his commitment. There are many times in life when you simply have to pack it in, lick your wounds, take your losses, and get out of there. For me, this was one of them.

Producing a Broadway musical, however, was not a dream I intended to give up on, despite advice to the contrary—which I received from everyone I knew in show business. My one enthusiastic supporter was my wife, Five. When John Denver bowed out, I got on the phone to Mac Davis, a very strong performer and someone I thought would make a terrific Will Rogers. I sent the book and the score to him and to his manager, Sandy Gallin. To my surprise, they both thought it was lousy and turned it down.

Starting in October of 1989, Tommy, Peter, Cy, Betty, Adolph, and I set up a series of auditions in New York for the role of Will Rogers. No one we saw was acceptable. Five had been bugging me to try Keith Carradine, but I didn't think he was right for the part. At her urging, however, I had a long meeting with Keith—who had been on Broadway in *Hair* and *Foxfire*—and I came away from it with the feeling that Five might be right after all. I called everyone and asked them to assemble once again to audition Keith Carradine. I flew from Los Angeles to New York with Keith, his lasso, and his guitar in hand. Everybody flipped out at his audition performance, and at last we had our star.

Now, I had to deal with the hard part. I needed $6,250,000 to produce the show, and at that point I had raised only $300,000: $200,000 from my friends Lisette and Norman Ackerberg, and $100,000 from my friend Richard Cohen. Both of them believed in what I was doing, and they had put up their money without even seeing the script or hearing the music. But I still needed $5,950,000 to complete the capitalization!

A month later, on November 28, 1989, I set up a backers' audition at 21. In attendance were 132 of the Broadway's biggest investors and theater owners. I said a few opening words, and then I turned the audition over to the team. Author Peter Stone read the Will Rogers part, Betty Comden did Betty Rogers, Adolph Green did Clem Rogers, and Cy Coleman read all the other parts. Not only was I certain that I'd come away with most of the money I needed, but I was also sure that the theater owners would bid against each other for the show. Imagine my surprise when only one investor emerged: William E. Simon, the former secretary of the U.S. Treasury. He loved it, so he put in $200,000. But for me, it was one of life's darker moments. I had $5,750,000 to go.

On January 26, 1990, I forged ahead and scheduled a second backers' audition, this time at Manhattan's plush Regency Hotel. Once again, I'd invited many heavy-hitters, including Roger Berlind, Nick Vanoff, and Herb Siegel. This audition resulted in a $100,000 investment from Herb Siegel's wife, Ann. Now the figure I had to come up with was a mere $5,650,000.

On April 4, 1990, I held a third backers' audition, at the Dramatists Guild Theater, next door to Sardi's. Once again, I had gathered one-hundred-plus heavy-hitters. The only taker was James Nederlander, who offered me one million, if I would contract to use a Nederlander theater—specifically, the Gershwin. What happened next illustrates what I said about there being no producers on Broadway.

My insistence on using the Gershwin was vetoed by the others. It started with Tommy Tune, to whom I had given "approval of theater" in his contract. He said no to the Gershwin, and the others followed suit. They insisted on the Palace, where the seating capacity was 1,200, as opposed to 2,000 at the Gershwin; this would have an enormous impact on our potential revenues. However, they all insisted on the Palace, and I was stuck with that decision. This was a major mistake, and it cost me dearly.

Although Jimmy Nederlander was disappointed about the Gershwin, he agreed to go along with the Palace. He had a partner in the Palace, Stuart Lane, and he wanted me to meet him. We met, and everything seemed to be set. Stuart wanted to come to the next backers' audition, which I thought was only natural. Fortunately, I had already planned a fourth backers' audition for May 4, 1990, at the Dramatists Guild Theater, so I didn't have to arrange a special audition for Lane. Several wealthy prospects in from Detroit, two Japanese companies, and Warner Brothers, Columbia, and MGM—all in all, another eighty-five people—came to this audition. This time, I didn't secure one red cent. Worse still, the next day Jimmy Nederlander called to say that Stuart Lane didn't like the show and wouldn't have it in the Palace!

By now, I had put on four backers' auditions, inviting anybody who was anybody in the world of Broadway-theater investing, and I had tapped every theater owner in New York. I had spent tons of my own money just getting up to the $600,000 mark. It was now May 5, 1990, and I was still $5,650,000 short. What a perfect time to say to myself "Don't throw good money after bad" and give up. Instead, I decided to do one more backers' audition—at the Tavern on the Green in Central Park. I would have professional performers replace Peter, Cy, Betty, and Adolph, and I would fly Keith Carradine in from Los Angeles. Cy Coleman arranged for Dee Hoty, who was then starring in his *City of Angels*, to play Will Rogers's wife. The last of New York's heavy-hitters were in attendance. Was I nervous? A little bit. Whoever said "There's no business like show business" was right.

Stuart Lane reversed his position and said we could use the Palace Theater. Although we'd been turned down by several Japanese companies at the four previous auditions, Mitchie Takeuchi of Japanese Satellite Broadcasting was suddenly very interested, as were others. Now comes the fun part. Tommy Tune was committed to start his road tour of *Bye Bye Birdie*, and I would absolutely not go forward without Tommy. If we couldn't fit the project into his time frame, I would have to either abort it or wait more than a year until he became available. Tommy simplified things even further, saying to me simply and unequivocally, "If I can't start by November 16, I can't do the show."

The scramble began. At my personal expense, I rented the Nederlander Theater on 44th Street, and we moved in on October 29, 1990. We started casting calls. I ordered the construction of rehearsal sets, and I tore through the zillion other preliminaries necessary to meet the November 16 target date. At my request, superagent Sam Cohn, who represented Peter, Cy, Betty, Adolph, and Tommy, set up a final do-or-die meeting for November 15th at International Creative Management in New York City. I was still the show's only producer, and I somehow had to raise $4,650,000.

On November 13, I called Keith Carradine in Los Angeles and told him not to come to New York for the November 16th rehearsal until he heard from me. He asked if there was a problem, and I hedged. Besides our crew (Cy Coleman, Peter Stone, Betty Comden, and Adolph Green), attending the meeting were: Mitchie Takeuchi of Japanese Satellite Broadcasting; Marty Richards and Sam Crothers of Producers Circle; Max Weitzenhoffer, who was known as a "Broadway angel"; Seth Gelblum, an attorney representing the show; Richard Harris, representing me; Floria Lasky, attorney for Producers Circle; Marvin Krauss, general manager of *The Will Rogers Follies*; James Nederlander; Stuart Lane; and assorted others. Back at the Nederlander Theater, Tony Walton continued to sketch set designs, Willa Kim worked up the costumes, and Tommy Tune conducted rehearsals.

I'll spare you the details of our all-day negotiations at International Creative Management, but I will tell you that I went into the meeting as the show's lone producer, having raised only $1,600,000, and I came out as one of seven producers, having raised $6,250,000. Here is the breakdown: Japanese Satellite Broadcasting, $2,000,000; Producers Circle, $1,000,000; Max Weitzenhoffer, $500,000; Pierre Cossette, $1,150,000; Palace Theater (previously committed), $1,000,000; Norman Ackerberg (previously committed), $200,000; William E. Simon (previously committed), $200,000; Ann Siegel (previously committed), $100,000; Richard Cohen (previously committed), $100,000. Total: $6,250,000.

Some of these commitments came with quid pro quos. Japanese Satellite Broadcasting received the rights to televise the show for Japan only. Jimmy Nederlander and Stuart Lane got a handsome Palace Theater lease. Producers Circle got sixteen of my offering points (the FCC allows thirty-two) in order to sell off their investment to third parties. This last one bothered me a bit, because it signaled to me that the Circle members did not totally believe in the show. There was no way I'd sell off any of my $1,150,000 investment—my gut feeling was that the show would be a smash hit.

I have to add that my good friend media mogul Jerry Perenchio did actually offer to buy three points, worth $600,000, provided he didn't have to read the script, hear the score, go to rehearsals, or attend opening night. I turned him down. The week before we opened, veteran Broadway producer Sander Jacobs offered me $500,000 for twenty-five percent of my share, and I turned him down too. Jacobs told me that it was the first time anyone had declined such an offer from him. Turning down that $1.1 million proved to be a bonanza for me: it left my generous piece of the pie intact.

I charged out of that International Creative Management meeting, grabbed a cab, and went straight to the Nederlander Theater. It was late in the day, and Tommy and the others looked despondent; by this time they were certain our project was a no go. One of the happiest moments in my long show business career was when I announced to them all, "It's a go!"

Although my ego suffered a bit because I was no longer the show's sole producer, I did remain the sole general partner. And it became obvious that I could never have put on *The Will Rogers Follies* without massive financial help. I was already stretched: my total investment thus far was $1,150,000, to say nothing of seven years' worth of hard work, and $250,000 in nonrecoupable expenses.

We completed the workshop and rehearsals and moved, ice cold (no out-of-town tryouts), into the Palace Theater, where we opened on April 1, 1991, for four weeks of previews. We lost quite a bit of money that month due to unforeseen costs involved in loading the production into a newly equipped and redecorated theater; plus, the box office for the preview period was disappointing. However, I still wasn't prepared for the night of April 10, when the show's general manager, Marvin Krauss, pulled me into the backstage production office, locked the door behind him, and said, "We need $750,000 by Monday afternoon or we'll have to post a closing notice on Monday night." This was Wednesday, and Monday was just three working days away.

After screaming at Marvin for giving me such short notice, I set up a meeting for the Friday—April 12—at the Embassy Hotel, next door to the Palace. In attendance were the producers and their various legal representatives. After a lengthy negotiation, I agreed to put up $500,000, and the other investors agreed to make up the remaining $250,000, but only after exacting more pieces of my pie. A short time later, I injected $100,000 more, and the others also pitched in again.

Then, success. We opened on May 1, 1991, the day before Tommy Tune had to leave town for his *Bye Bye Birdie* tour, and we took off. Eventually, we won six Tony Awards, more than any other show, including the award for Best Musical, and that was against formidable competition such as *Miss Saigon*. We also won the Drama Critics' Award plus the Drama Desk Award, and later, we scored a Grammy for Best Broadway Cast Album. I accepted that Tony for Best Musical on June 1. I can't remember a word I said, except that I was careful to introduce my six coproducers, who stood behind me.

The show had run for ten months when Keith Carradine said to me, "I'd like to leave after this first year and take the show on the road." This was good news and bad news. Good, because he wanted to go on the road, and few Broadway stars ever do. Bad, because there was no replacing him in the Broadway production—he played the role to perfection. But that was that.

We had to set up audition schedules to find Keith's replacement. At this time, I was producing the Grammy Awards at Radio City Music Hall. Two days before that show, a surprise visitor came into my production office. It was John Denver, who said, "Pierre, I've seen *The Will Rogers Follies* two nights in a row, and you've got to let me replace Keith Carradine when he leaves."

"Got to?" I was hysterical with joy. I called the writers and told them we had John Denver. They, too, were ecstatic. I got on the phone with John Denver's agent at the William Morris Agency. After two weeks of negotiation, we learned that John Denver could not afford to cancel his state fairs and concerts through June, July, and August. His final position was that he'd only take the role if he could rehearse in September and start in October. We couldn't accommodate that, so, unfortunately, we had to pass on John Denver.

Once again, we set to work arranging more Keith Carradine replacement auditions. At about this time, I was playing golf in California when who do I run into but my old friend Mac Davis. Jokingly, I said, "Mac, would you like to replace Keith Carradine in *The Will Rogers Follies*?" We both laughed, knowing how negative

Mac had been when I first offered him the deal. But, you guessed it: two days later, I get a call from Mac. He says, "Pierre, I've been thinking about your invite. My wife, Lisa, thinks I should do it. Can we talk about it?"

Mac and I went to the Hollywood Roosevelt Hotel to meet with Tommy Tune, who was in L.A. for one day only. The meeting went well, and one week later, Mac Davis was in New York rehearsing his heart out. We opened May 1, 1992, and Mac was absolutely sensational. The touring production, starring the original cast—Keith Carradine and Dee Hoty—opened August 25 in San Francisco, and it was soon booked two years in advance.

Under the Broadway system, my producing duties ended the day Tommy Tune, Peter Stone, Cy Coleman, Betty Comden, and Adolph Green were contracted to write, direct, and compose the music for the show. All rights and ownership then reverted to them. It was like losing a child. I no longer had a say in anything—whether it was adding or cutting a song or a production number, or changing the show's conceptual direction. Although the creators could allow me to license the rights from them for a limited time, I was prohibited from making movie or TV deals; I did, however, receive my share of the profits. The only exclusive rights I retained were to tour the show worldwide as a Broadway musical. Nevertheless, as the sole general partner, I remained financially responsible for the entire package. Simply put, any losses incurred or lawsuits filed came out of my pocket. Not an easy business.

Jimmy Nederlander insisted that I was the man to produce the Tony Awards. I'd had it with Broadway by that point, so I told him that unless I could make substantial changes to the show I wasn't interested. Jimmy wouldn't give up. He arranged for the Tony Awards committee to meet with me, saying, "You're a shoe-in. They'd love to have you. The meeting is just a formality." What did I have to lose? I went to the meeting and was greeted by the board of directors of the American Theater Wing—each member had produced big hits—and Isabelle Stevenson, the longtime president of the Antoinette Perry Awards, better known as the Tonys.

After the opening rituals, we took our seats. Isabelle started by saying, "We'd like your ideas on producing the Tony Awards." I said, "Anybody in this room can produce the show. A producer is the last thing you need. What you need is to put this show on the map. It should be twice as important as it is now, and it should attract a much larger audience. You're sitting in the media capital of the world with a Broadway identity, which is as institutionalized as a Hollywood identity; and Broadway is, in fact, the granddaddy of everything that's been happening in show business for decades. In other words, you have a diamond that you treat like a peanut." I kept going, full-tilt: "Your preopening party should be at a large Broadway house with a fabulous show, depicting the history of Broadway, with fifty stars, new and old. Charge five hundred dollars a ticket and make a donation to charity or some worthy causes in the theater circuit."

I paused. I was just warming up. Isabelle abruptly excused herself, saying she had forgotten that she had another appointment. And that was the end of the idea that Pierre Cossette should produce the Tony Awards. In other words, they changed their minds. I still believe everything I said in that meeting, and I feel the same way about the Academy Awards. That enterprise suffers from the same laissez-faire attitude as the Tonys. If anyone would let me (and they wouldn't), I'd produce the Oscar telecast from Madison Square Garden. It would be the best thing that could happen to the Academy Awards.

Not long after this, when I'd gotten over being fed up with Broadway, a great idea occurred to me: a Broadway "Ballet Sinatra" featuring Frank Sinatra recordings. A troupe of ballet dancers would do silhouette performances in front of, and behind, scrims (see-through curtains). The project would require a top-notch sound system—something totally new for Broadway—with forty speakers positioned throughout the theater. And to accomplish what I envisioned, I'd need a good lighting system and graphics to blend with the talent. Excited, I sent an elaborate proposal to Frank. A week later, his letter arrived: "Dear Pierre, No!—Francis." I never said you could win them all.

At the Grammy Awards rehearsal in 1991, I sat having lunch alone in the middle of Radio City Music Hall. A sheet of plywood was balanced on the seats in front of me, and it was laden with TV monitors, earphones, and other gear. Right up until show time, it would serve as my production desk. The marquee out front read, "Thirty-Second Annual Grammy Awards. A Pierre Cossette Production."

As I ate my sandwich, I started to contemplate how I had gotten here. Suddenly, my recollections were shattered by a loud voice from the balcony: "Throw a light on the Austrian!" I looked at the stage, glanced around the theater, then grabbed my sheet to find out who'd booked an Austrian on the show. I was still rummaging through my papers when the shout came again: "Throw a light on the Austrian!"

I was already working myself up to fire the person responsible for booking this "Austrian" without my permission when, once more from the balcony and louder than ever, the voice boomed: "*Hey!* Put a light on the Austrian!" I knew that none of the talent would be back for an hour, so I hollered back, "He won't be here till three!" Then I settled back into my little internal retrospective.

That afternoon, the stage manager came to me and said, "The union guys want to add six more stagehands."

"Why?" I sputtered.

"They said if the producer doesn't know what a curtain is, how can he know what's going on backstage?"

What I hadn't realized was that the curtain circling the proscenium is known as the "Austrian." After some forty years in the business, I can still pull a blooper like that one. My son John said, "Pop, I can't believe you did that!" The guys at Radio City still kid me about it.

The Grammy Awards requires an army of eighteen stage managers, 150 stagehands, 120 technicians, and six hundred musicians, dancers, and extras—to say nothing of all the security personnel in the wake of the 9/11 tragedy. Over 275,000 pounds of lighting and sound equipment hang from the ceiling above the two stages. One thousand microphones and nine computerized audio boards stand by. To put this in perspective, a big Broadway musical requires three stage managers, forty stagehands, and maybe two dozen technicians.

In October of 1994, I got a call from Frank and Kathie Lee Gifford, inviting me to meet them for lunch. I had known Frank from my USC days, when I beat him out as "Mr. Trojanality." Later, I met Kathie Lee and came to adore her. At lunch, Frank explained that they had a deal with CBS for Kathie Lee to do a Christmas special, and part of the deal was that they engage a top production company to deliver the show. CBS had recommended a few, and Pierre Cossette Productions was on their list. Frank and Kathie Lee asked me if I'd do it, and I happily accepted.

One night, Five and I went to Frank and Kathie Lee's home for dinner. The only other couple the Giffords had invited was Donald

Trump and Marla Maples. I knew Donald quite well, but I'd never met Marla. I sat opposite her at the dinner table, and we talked it up and had a great time. At some point—I guess the notion had been stirring in the back of my mind—I said to her, "You'd be terrific in *The Will Rogers Follies*."

"I would?" she said.

"Absolutely."

"Which part?"

"Ziegfeld's Favorite."

"That's a great role."

"Yes, and Kady Huffman, the girl who's been doing the part for the past couple of years is leaving the show."

Immediately, Marla informed the others that I wanted her to star in *The Will Rogers Follies*. Everybody had a laugh over it, and that was it. A few days later, Marla called and asked, "Were you serious about me doing *The Will Rogers Follies*?" When I told her I was, she said, "Then let's talk. I might be interested if you really think I can do it."

Now, here's where my early experience booking and staging nightclub acts came into play. I'd learned that you don't have to be a dancer to dance, and you don't have to be an actress to act. What you need is a role that can accommodate as little or as much talent as you can bring to it. Although I saw Marla as someone who could be molded into a star, there was still one enormous stumbling block. I had handed over cast approval to Cy Coleman, Betty Comden, Adolph Green, Peter Stone, and Tommy Tune; and I knew I'd hit a stone wall if I asked them to consider casting Marla Maples. Not one of them would want to touch it. So my only hope was to let them see for themselves—I had to convince them to audition her.

I called Philip Osterman, an assistant director for the show, and begged him to work with Marla on the part in secret. Next, I went to assistant choreographer Patti De Beck and asked her to work through the dance moves with Marla. While this was going on, I worked on getting the others to come to Marla's audition. Six weeks after Marla had started working with Phil and Patti, she was ready to audition. What a day! The media got word of it and tried to crash the audition, but we managed to keep them out. Marla sang the songs and did all the struts and the dances in cowboy boots and hat. As she was performing, I was nervously trying to read the faces around me.

When the audition was over, no one said a word. Each person was waiting for someone else to break the ice. Cy Coleman was the first to speak. He said, "Marla, would you be willing to work with me on the music for a couple of weeks and then come back and audition again?" She said she was, and I said to myself, "Bingo! She's got the part." Cy is as tough a taskmaster as they come, at least on Broadway. His willingness to work with Marla was an indication to me that she'd get the part. And she did.

The Will Rogers Follies had already been on Broadway for twenty-seven months when Marla joined the cast. On her opening night, however, neither the seasoned cast nor I were ready for what happened. More TV crews and paparazzi gathered outside the theater than Broadway had ever seen before, and we had to delay the start of the show.

Finally, we got under way. The show's opening number is called "Willamania." Not only is it a very difficult song to perform, but it's also one of the biggest production numbers in the show. We knew that if Marla could get through it, the rest would be smooth sailing. As the overture played, neither Marla nor I could help thinking about the fact that every critic in New York City was out there waiting to rip her to shreds, call the whole thing a gimmick, pronounce her "Trump's, not Ziegfeld's, favorite." I was sitting there with my heart in my throat as Marla came up through the floor on the elevator that delivered her to the stage. Wearing chaps, a ten-gallon hat, and a lethal look, she stared down the audience, fierce as Wyatt Earp. She dared them not to like her.

It worked, and I must say that I shed a little tear. I understood what Marla was going through. I'd seen much the same thing with Ann-Margret when everybody called her a no-talent and predicted that she'd never make it in show business. Well, Ann-Margret did make it, and she made it big. The disaster reviews everybody expected for Marla didn't materialize; instead, she won good reviews, and even some excellent ones. Tickets for the show became scarce. Marla was a smash. She'd done it, and she deserved all the credit and adulation that it brought her.

Two weeks after Marla's opening, I was playing golf with Donald Trump. "Pierre," he said, "You really took a big gamble bringing Marla into your show. She'd never been on a stage in her life. She could have bombed and closed you down. That was a high-risk situation."

I thanked him and said, "I know I was really rolling the dice, but I had a gut feeling it was the right thing to do."

"Well it was, and you're to be congratulated. And, by the way, now that she's a big hit, she'd like more money."

We laughed, and we never mentioned it again. Naturally, rumors spread that Marla got the part because Donald Trump put up the money. But he didn't—not one thin dime. He did, however, back her emotionally.

In this business, you get blasé. Nothing seems completely real, and very little fazes you. For example, Marla was our houseguest in Malibu for three weeks. Donald stayed with us for a few days, but he was out most of the time. Five had to go to Colorado for four days to be with her two daughters, who were attending school there, and that, of course, meant that I was alone with Marla. (It reminded me of the good old days, when every man's dream was to spend a few nights with Betty Grable.) When I told people I was living alone with Marla Maples, they either said "poor Marla" or refused to believe me.

Donald Trump never ceases to amaze me. During the U.S. Open Golf Tournament in New Jersey, we took off in his helicopter from Manhattan's waterfront heliport and landed on the edge of the tournament golf course, where a four-passenger security golf cart picked us up and took us to the Donald Trump party tent. Many of the top five hundred companies have these tents. We'd watch the tournament on TV in the tent and then hop into the golf cart and go out to where the best action was. We did this for three days. On the last day, we followed the late Payne Stewart and Lee Jantzen. On the seventeenth tee, Jantzen and Stewart were neck and neck. As it turned out, Lee Jantzen became the new U.S. Open champ.

When they putted out on the eighteenth green, Donald turned the cart towards the clubhouse. I said, "Hey, Donald, we'll never get in there. It's a zoo, and it's members only." He said, "Stick with me." Passing four "Players Only" signs, we ended up in the shower area, where we found Payne Stewart, stark naked. He looked up and said, "Hey, Donald, what's happening?" Donald said, "I want you to meet my friend Pierre Cossette." We shook hands. Now, I've gone to lots of golf tournaments, and I've never gotten near the locker-room; suddenly, here I am, shaking hands in a shower with a bare-assed Payne Stewart, who ten minutes before had missed a putt and lost the U.S. Open before sixty million viewers worldwide.

Flying back to New York in the helicopter, I said, "Donald, you absolutely amaze me. How do you get away with having a golf cart at the U.S. Open, landing your helicopter alongside the course, and passing through enormous security right into the players' shower room?"

"Let's put it this way: I'm the largest taxpayer in the state of New Jersey."

I love show business!

In 1993, I was negotiating with the Lawrence Welk Theater in Branson, Missouri, to book *The Will Rogers Follies*. Branson is like a mini Las Vegas; several major stars are working there all the time. It was a natural for *The Will Rogers Follies*. I signed Branson's favorite, Pat Boone, to play the role of Will Rogers, and we were off and running. Until, that is, I received a call from Lee Iacocca, who said he was buying extensive acreage in Branson to build a hotel, apartment, and real estate complex around a theater. He wanted my show to open his operation. I had known Lee for a long time, and by now he was an American icon. So I cut off my negotiations with the Lawrence Welk people and got into business with Lee Iacocca.

My friends Andy Williams, Bobby Vinton, and Tony Orlando all owned theaters in Branson, and they assured me that *Will Rogers* would be a big hit there. The show had been touring for two and a half years, and it was an enormous hit on the road—although, inexplicably, it didn't hit in Boston. After we opened in Branson, it became apparent that it wasn't going to hit there, either. I was shocked and disappointed.

I'd also lost $310,000 on the undertaking, because I'd incurred some hefty expenses in anticipation of a hit. For one thing, I flew Lee and his partner by private jet from Palm Springs to Branson to see the show. Commercial airlines could not land in Branson, only in Springfield. The drive from Springfield to Branson was an hour and a half, so to show off my importance I chartered a Lear jet to land in Branson. It was a great idea, except for the fact that the airport in Branson closed due to bad weather, and we had to land in Springfield.

After *The Will Rogers Follies*, I produced a show called *Tommy Tune Tonite*. From there, I went on to produce two major musicals: *The Scarlet Pimpernel* and *The Civil War*. Each was nominated for a Tony for Best Musical—*The Scarlet Pimpernel* in 1998, and *The Civil War* in 1999. In 1998, we were beaten by *The Lion King*; and in 1999, we lost to *Fosse*, which pissed me off, because *Fosse* should never have been allowed to compete as an original.

One day back in 1987, I was sitting in my summer home in St. Anicet, Quebec, browsing through the local papers. I read something about a singer who was appearing at a nearby nightclub—a nice, six-hundred-seat nightclub. The singer's name was Céline Dion. I had already heard about her; she was a Sony recording artist, and she was beginning to make a bit of noise.

As producer of the Grammys and variety specials, I always tried to keep up with new developments in the music business, so I made a point of going to see Céline. She absolutely knocked me out. I went backstage and met with her and her manager (and future husband), René Angelil, and their associate Ben Kaye. I found out that Céline was with CAA (I also learned that Ben and René's association dates back to 1961, when Ben managed René, who was a member of Les Baronets, a popular singing group). CAA was the biggest agency in Hollywood, and it was run by Mike Ovitz, somebody you might have heard of. So I wrote a letter to Mike: "Dear Mike: Your agency is representing a girl I think is the next Streisand. I doubt that your agents are aware of her, except those in the variety and concert departments, but she is absolutely sensational, and you should nurture her because you have a great, great property there." I sent a copy of that letter to René and Céline, and, of course, they were ever grateful for it.

A year later, Céline was nominated for a Grammy Award, but there were about five names on the nomination list, all of whom could attract a larger television audience—they were all pretty big stars. This Céline Dion girl was from Canada, and the mass American audience didn't know her. However, the Grammys was my show, so I put her on, and once again she was a knockout. She's since done several Grammy telecasts. That was the beginning story of my relationship with Céline and René.

Later, when Sony wanted Céline to do a CBS special, they hired my production company for the job because of previous relationships. I went on to produce three Céline Dion CBS television specials, but the first was one of the most wonderful specials I've ever been connected with. The production traveled to Céline's Quebec hometown, where she was raised with her thirteen brothers and sisters in an unbelievably small house. By this time, Céline was a superstar, but to the local people she was simply Céline. There were no crowds, no groupies, no autographs, and I found that to be very, very refreshing. But the most refreshing thing of all was the Dion family. I fell in love with them; they are wonderful people.

Papa Dion could have been Bob Hope. He really has a great style—he's smart and lovable. He told me a joke in French, then he told me to tell him one. I came up with one that everybody would understand, and Papa brought a few of his pals and a couple of his sons over to hear it. My joke was about a man who's set to give the most important speech of his life, and half an hour before he's supposed to deliver it, he loses his voice. He doesn't know what to do. So somebody says, "We'll get an interpreter." The man is introduced, and he stands up in front of four thousand people, the interpreter at his side. He pantomimes a lady with big breasts and hips. The interpreter says, "Ladies." Then he pantomimes a man by raising his arms to show his muscles and tweaking his moustache. The interpreter says, "and gentlemen." Next, he pantomimes that he is masturbating. The interpreter says, "It gives me great pleasure . . ."

Now, Papa Dion went absolutely crazy. He thought it was the funniest joke he had every heard. That night, we were at a famous studio in the hinterlands of Quebec recording some things for the show. The whole family was there. All the locals were there. I noticed Papa going around doing a masturbating motion with his hand. I told Céline to tell Papa that it's okay to tell the joke, but he didn't have to make that motion so flagrantly. She just said, "Well, you know Papa."

Anyway, we taped segments of the show and returned to L.A. to finish it. It was just magic. Céline and René desperately wanted to have a singer they knew make a guest appearance on the show. I'd never heard of this performer, who happened to be from Italy. Today, everyone knows him: Andrea Bocelli. I soon discovered that the man was a great singer and an absolutely beautiful human being. I asked him if he ever did any of the Broadway show tunes. "No," he replied, "but I will do something nonoperatic for you," and he started doing Sinatra. Over the years, I've heard a lot of singers do Sinatra impersonations, but I never heard anything like this. It was so right on. Bocelli did "Come Fly with Me" and a couple of other tunes, and when he was done I walked away with deep admiration for the man.

After the success of *The Will Rogers Follies*, I wanted to do another musical, and soon. In my early days at MCA, I'd developed a fondness for country music, so I organized a tour of the Capitol Records country stars. We called it Capitol's Caravan of Stars, and it was a huge hit. And in 1973, I produced the Grammy Awards from a downtown Nashville motion picture house. Add to this the fact that Glenn Rose, president of Acuff/Rose, was also president of the

Recording Academy, and you can see where my interest in country music came from.

When it came to mounting my second Broadway musical, I was passionate about doing *Hank*, the story of Hank Williams, the most prolific writer and performer in country music history. His string of crossover and country hits was as long as his affection for booze, broads, and drugs was deep. I was very aware of Hank Williams and his many hits, because in the sixties I'd managed George Hamilton, and I'd talked George into playing the Hank Williams part in the very successful MGM movie *The Hank Williams Story*.

And so I made a date with the good ol' boys at Acuff/Rose in Nashville and presented my idea for *Hank*, the Broadway musical— I had to obtain the music rights from them before I could go ahead. We had two or three meetings, and they finally said to me, fondly, "Go ahead. We like your idea, and we know you'll take care of ol' Hank." Acuff/Rose set me up with members of Hank's early band. They told me they were excited because I would be bringing international recognition to their library of Hank Williams songs.

The good 'ol boys invited me to dinner to celebrate the occasion. During that dinner, one of them said, "You know, when I first came to Nashville many years ago, I was broke. All I could afford to buy the missus was flour sacks for dresses. She wore flour-sack blouses, flour-sack skirts, flour-sack bras, and flour-sack panties." This story interested me, and I was eager for him to continue. I knew it must have something to do with Hank Williams. "Today," he said, "I'm a very wealthy man, but I'll tell you one thing: every time I eat a biscuit I get a hard-on!" I exploded with laughter, not so much at the joke itself but at the way he delivered it. I thought he was just telling me a wonderful story, and I never saw the punch line coming.

I hired a terrific writer for my musical: Bill Kerby. He had written hit movies such as *The Rose*, which starred Bette Midler, and he was a tremendous country music fan. After three months, he brought me an absolutely brilliant play. It was what I had dreamed of, and I could feel the Tony Award coming towards me for the second time, on my second try. I could have gotten any star to play the lead. I was in heaven, and I sent the script to Nashville for Acuff/Rose's approval. Their reaction changed my life.

The good ol' boys read the play and said, "Ol' Hank didn't do that . . . ol' Hank used to drink, but ol' Hank never took drugs . . . and ol' Hank was never a womanizer." The more they said about "ol' Hank," the clearer it became that my dreams would not come true, because I refused to whitewash Hank's life story and use it as a vehicle to punch up their song catalogue. It was either my way or the highway. I would not compromise, and neither would they. Unfortunately, I did not have a signed contract. They had assured me that in their neck of the woods a handshake was all that was necessary.

I had read several books and a lot of other material on Hank Williams, and I knew that every detail of my play was accurate. Too bad—just another day in showbiz.

My Way

THE 1994 GRAMMY AWARDS, held at Radio City Music Hall, earned worldwide press coverage. We'd purportedly cut off Frank Sinatra in the middle of his acceptance speech, and the whole thing was a fiasco. But here's what really happened.

Bono of U2 was to present the Grammy Living Legend Award to Frank Sinatra, an honor that had previously gone to Paul McCartney and later Barbra Streisand. It was agreed that Bono would write his own intro, a task usually given to the show's head writer. We were concerned, because up to the day of the show, we had not received any material from Bono, despite our repeated requests.

Then, at 2:00 in the afternoon of the telecast, Bono asked director Walter Miller and me to join him in the hall's last row of seats. Miller and I sat down on either side of Bono, who was typing on his laptop computer. "Wait a few minutes," he said. "I've got to finish this." When he finished, he told us that we could read it if we promised that it wouldn't go on the teleprompter, where other people could see it, and that it wouldn't go into the script. He would memorize it, and that would be it. We agreed. I read it, and I thought it was a perfect tribute from the leader of the young guard to the leader of the old guard. Walter Miller felt the same.

That night, Frank Sinatra waited backstage to receive his honor, unable to hear what Bono was saying about him. He had asked to see the script and was told that there was none. This is how the lead-in to the presentation went:

> *Garry Shandling*: And now, ladies and gentlemen, to present the Lifetime Achievement Award to Frank Sinatra, please give a welcome to Bono.
>
> *Bono*: Right. Frank never did like rock and roll. And he's not crazy about guys wearing earrings either. But he doesn't hold it against me in any way. The feeling is not mutual. Rock and roll people love Frank Sinatra, because Frank Sinatra has got what we want: swagger and attitude. He's big on attitude. Serious attitude. Bad attitude. Frank's the Chairman of the Bad. Rock and roll plays at being tough, but this guy, well, he's the boss. The boss of bosses. The man. The big bang of pop. Who's this guy that every city in America wants to claim as their own? This painter who lives in the desert? The first-rate, first-take actor? This singer who makes other men poets, boxing clever with every word, talking like America, fast, straight up, in headlines, coming through with the big shtick, the aside, the quiet compliments, good cop/bad cop, all in the same breath? You know his story, cause it's your story. Frank walks like America, cop-sure. It's 1945, and the U.S. Cavalry are trying to get their asses out of Europe, but they never really do. They're part of another kind of invasion. AF, or American Forces radio, broadcasting a music that'll curl the stiff upper lip of England, and the rest of the world, paving the way for rock and roll with jazz, Duke

Ellington, Tommy Dorsey, and, right out in front, Frank Sinatra, his voice tight as a fist, opening at the end of a bar, not on the beat, over it, playing with it, splitting it, like a jazz man. Like Miles Davis, turning on the right phrase and the right sound, which is where he lives, where he lets go, where he reveals himself. His songs are home, and he lets you in. But you know, to sing like that, you've got to have lost a couple of fights. To know tenderness and romance, you've got to have had your heart broken. People say Frank hasn't talked to the press. They want to know how he is. What's on his mind. But, you know, Sinatra's out there more nights than most punk bands, selling his story through the songs. Telling and articulating in the choice of those songs. Private thoughts, on a public address system . . . generous. This is the conundrum of Frank Sinatra, left and right brain hardly talking, boxer and painter, actor and singer, lover and father, band man and loner, troubleshooter and troublemaker, the champ who would rather show you his scars than his medals. He may be putty in Barbara's hands, but I'm not going to mess with him. Are you? Ladies and gentlemen, are you ready to welcome a man heavier than the Empire State, more connected than the Twin Towers, as recognizable as the Statue of Liberty, and living proof that God is a Catholic? Will you welcome the king of New York City, Francis Albert Sinatra?

The curtain split, and out walked Frank Sinatra to one of the most stunning ovations ever seen in New York City. He was totally overwhelmed. He'd told us that he would do a couple of the lines he used to close his concerts and then walk off. But he was so taken aback by the ovation that he became very emotional and responded this way instead:

Frank Sinatra: That's the best welcome . . . I ever had. This is like being in baseball—the bases are loaded, and you're at bat. You don't know what you're gonna do. Isn't that pretty? I can use this [pointing to his Grammy] when the wind blows; it won't blow me away anymore with this thing here. It's quite beautiful. Ladies and gentlemen, I'm delighted to see you all. If we do this again, I'm not leaving you yet, but if we do it again from time to time, and I get to see you and get to know some of you, it's important to me, it's very important to me. This is more applause than Dean heard in his whole career. He used to keep one guy in the audience to keep it going all the time, you know. I don't know what went on while you were out here. Were there performances here on stage? Good. I hope you weren't out there drinking all night and didn't ask me to come and join you. Very dry back there. Not one guy said, "Would you like a little nip?" Then a girl came by: "A little water, Mr. Sinatra?" Ha, I'll give you a whack right in the mouth. I'm looking for my girl, where's my girl? There she is. Say hello to Barbara, everybody, please. There she is. That's my girl. I love you. You love me? I love you twice. I don't quite know what to say to you. There were no discussions about singing a couple of songs, otherwise if we had, there would be an orchestra here with me. But apparently that's not what they wanted tonight, and I'm angry. I'm hurt. I'm just happy to be here in the Apple, I love coming back all the time—it's the best city in the whole world.

This is where we cut him off. We were stunned when the next day when every headline in America screamed, "Sinatra Cut Off To Go To Commercial!" Was Frank Sinatra upset by this? Absolutely not. Was Barbara Sinatra upset by this? Absolutely not. Were Frank's management team and children upset by this? Absolutely not.

I've done a lot of things in this business, but I never produced a feature-length motion picture. It was not for lack of trying, however. In 1962, I bought Frances Ford Coppola's first screenplay, "Pilma." I still own it. I was never able to get it off the ground, because by 1964, its treatment of the topic—mental illness—was dated.

I did sell a movie to Paramount Pictures, however. It starred Jan and Dean, a hot rock and roll act of the late fifties and early sixties. On the first day of filming, we were working on a train-wreck scene, and something went wrong. The director was almost killed, and Jan suffered injuries that he never fully recovered from. With no director and one of our two stars out of commission, we had to cancel the project; we were never able to put it together again. It had a great musical score, and I know it would have been terrific.

A few years ago, an item appeared in Army Archerd's *Daily Variety* column that said Pierre Cossette was going into the feature film business. Army had learned that I'd bought the rights to best-selling author Jay McInerney's novel *Ransom* and had paid screenwriter James Dearden a substantial amount of money to do the screenplay. McInerney was a hot young novelist, and Dearden was a hot young screenwriter, having just written the big hit *Fatal Attraction*.

Not long after that, I got a call from superagent Mike Ovitz, who said, "Pierre, you can't get into the movie business. Stay out of it."

I said, "Why?"

He said, "You're going to screw it up for everybody."

"How?"

"Well, you've never screwed anybody in a deal. You don't know how to connive and in-fight and do what you have to do to be a picture producer. If you get into this end of the business, it will ruin it for the rest of us." He laughed loudly and hung up. It was Mike's way of wishing me well.

But then Bob Daly, chairman and CEO of Time-Warner and one of my closest friends, told me the same thing: "The film business is too rough-and-tumble for you, Pierre. You're successful at what you do. Making movies will use up ninety-five percent of your time, and you'll only be able to do one a year, at best."

This is probably very good advice, but I'm still going to get *Ransom* made into a movie and see what happens. It's the only thing left in show business that I haven't done, and I've got the urge, whether it's right for me or not. And I still have strong interest from a major studio. I won't say which one—that would invite bad luck. But by the time you read this book, you'll know whether my picture got off the ground or not. I also purchased rights to another book, at Five's urging. It's called *Buster Midnight's Cafe*. We've hired a writer, Susan McMartin, to do the screenplay. I think it's going to be terrific. I'll make it in the movie business yet—just you wait.

Deep in my heart, I have a soft spot for producing benefits and fundraisers. I've done many through the years, for every kind of cause. Among my favorites is the Concern Foundation for cancer research. A group of Beverly Hills doctors, including Dr. Wilbur Schwartz, my personal physician, established Concern, but they found they couldn't raise sufficient money to make it viable. So Dr. Schwartz got after me to produce a big fundraiser for them. He was giving me a physical exam when I rejected the idea—I was just too busy—but he had his finger up my ass, and he wouldn't remove it until I said yes. That was the beginning of Concern Foundation's real success.

I got the City of Beverly Hills to grant us access to Rodeo Drive for a twenty-four-hour period. The foundation's doctors and their friends showed up at daybreak, and we had everything ready for a 4:00 p.m. start. The concept was the Concern Foundation block party. We had movie stars up and down Rodeo Drive tending bar or running hot dog stands. Leading Beverly Hills restaurants provided the food. We erected a stage across Rodeo, just in front of the Beverly Hills Hotel, and we put on a great show for all to see. Over the years, those who show up at the block party have been treated to performances by the likes of Frank Sinatra, Don Rickles, Andy Williams, and Natalie Cole.

The Concern fundraiser is still up and running, but we had to move it from Rodeo Drive to the Paramount Studios back lot in order to accommodate more people. After fifteen years, I had to bow out, because the event had become too big for me to handle on my own. The young members of the Concern Foundation took over, and they're doing a great job. But I take pride in the fact that Concern has done great things for cancer research. I also take pride in the fact that the name of Rodeo Drive was changed to Cossette Drive— it was only for a day, but, oh, what a feeling!

Among my favorite all-time benefit shows was for the Los Angeles Suicide Prevention Center. Buddy Hackett came to me and said, "Pierre, my wife and I are on the board of the Suicide Prevention Center, and I promised them I would put on a huge fundraiser for them. I can't do it because I'm on the road ninety percent of the time, but I told them I'd ask you to do it. I'll help you book it by phone wherever I am. Between us, we'll put on a fabulous show." And we did. We booked every name you ever heard of, and it was a smash.

After the show, Buddy said, "That was great. Thanks for your help. By the way, the chairman of the Suicide Prevention Center wants to meet you and thank you." When Buddy introduced me to the chairman, I said, with great confidence, "How did you like the show?" The chairman replied, "The show was so bad I wanted to commit suicide." The gag was obviously set up by Buddy, but it proves that comedians know how to be funny.

Recently, I produced a benefit at New York's Avery Fisher Hall for the Society of Singers honoring Lena Horne on her eightieth birthday. Many stars performed that night, and I was so proud that Lena had chosen me to do it. Also, on November 14, 2001, I had the enormous pleasure of producing a show to mark the retirement of former New York mayor Rudolph Giuliani. Larry King hosted, and the show featured Bette Midler, Tony Bennett, and Natalie Cole; on hand for the proceedings were Mayor Michael Bloomberg and Governor George Pataki.

These days, I've been concentrating on producing industrial shows for major corporations. My company did the launch for the new Microsoft project in San Francisco. It's like doing a television special. We had all kinds of special effects and a big show featuring Santana. Bill Gates himself kicked off the evening.

The ad agency behind the event wanted the opening part of Gates's speech to be charming and witty, highlighting the true warmth of the man. I came up with the following: "I'm humbled by the exceptional warmth of your reception, but I must tell you that I do not deserve credit for inventing the Internet, or any other part of the computer world. To find those who do deserve the credit, you have to go all the way back to Adam and Eve. Eve had an Apple, and Adam had a Wang."

Some of the ad guys loved it, but most were too afraid to go with it. Later on, Bill Gates heard about it, and he said he would have loved to have done it. In the meantime, my son John, who is responsible for this division, said to me, "Pop, you should stay out of this corporate stuff—they don't think like you do."

We also introduced the American Express blue card by putting on a tremendous rock concert in New York's Central Park. We had Sheryl Crow, the Dixie Chicks, Eric Clapton, and many others. Backstage, I was a very proud father. John had not only produced this event, but he'd also picked the Central Park location and designed the set and the lighting. Twentieth Century Fox televised the show.

March 1, 1995, was a thrilling day for me. It was my twenty-fifth anniversary as producer of the Grammy Awards telecast, and the Recording Academy presented me with their Trustee's Award. I stood before one hundred million viewers worldwide and received my very own Grammy Award. It is mind-blowing to be awarded the same honor as greats like Cole Porter, George Gershwin, Frank Sinatra, and Duke Ellington.

It was also a very touching moment for me. I couldn't help thinking back to the time, twenty-five years before, when I'd had such trouble getting the Grammys on the air. Even after I'd managed to do that, the network canceled us in our third year. But we pulled ourselves together and got back in the game. We started out as a ninety-minute show, grew to two hours, and finally expanded to three hours. The growth curve has been enormous. I also remembered the contribution of Christine Farnon, to whom I owe deep thanks. Christine has never received the recognition she deserves for everything she did to make the Grammy Awards show the huge success that it has become. Finally, I thought about how privileged I was to have had the opportunity to start something that will live on for many years after I'm gone. I like to think that my great, great,

great grandchildren will be watching the Grammy Awards live on television.

A month after receiving that award, I attended the closing of Chasen's, the famous Beverly Hills restaurant. The whole world of show business was there. It was a wonderful night and a tearful night.

Again, my mind drifted back—this time to 1952, when Foopie and I first set foot in Chasen's. We were on a double date with Mike Meshekoff, the producer of *Dragnet*, TV's hottest show, and Foopie's friend Helena Carter. That night, the place was filled with movie stars, and even Foopie was in awe of Chasen's and what it stood for.

We used to talk about the day we could finally afford to have dinner at Chasen's. In fact, after we married, we kept a jar in the bedroom for what we called our "Chasen's fund." We'd put money into it whenever we could. As soon we had enough, we hauled ourselves off to Chasen's. We finally started making enough money to become Chasen's regulars—meaning, among other things, that we were led to the same booth every time we came. When Foopie was dying, the management of Chasen's prepared something special for her every night and delivered it to the hospital. She loved it.

A happier memory was the night we threw a party at Chasen's for fifty guests. Our guests were served Dom Perignon, caviar, and lobster. Next came crab. And then the maitre d' and several waiters rolled in serving carts bearing covered silver platters. When the waiters ceremoniously lifted the lids, our guests found themselves staring down at Swanson's TV dinners.

I also reminisced about the twenty years of Super Bowl parties I staged at Chasen's. About four hundred people generally showed up—a mixture of stars, executives, studio and network heads, agents, lawyers, managers, directors, producers, and what have you. We'd have huge TV screens mounted everywhere, and we'd serve hot dogs, hamburgers, French fries, ice cream bars, and popcorn. The only booze was beer and wine.

After twenty years, I moved the party to Sardi's, in the heart of New York's theater district. My friends said, "You moved your party to New York, and now they have to close Chasen's." Anyway, it was a walk down memory lane for a lot of us that night.

Looking Back

I WAS IN LAS VEGAS recently for the first time in many years. I was dumbstruck by all the changes that had occurred since my time there. In my MCA years, Vegas had a very small airport. At any one time, it could handle only two passenger planes; it had a two-man baggage crew and boasted a four-stool soda fountain. If you hopped a cab and drove down the entire Vegas strip, first you'd see the Flamingo on the right and the Last Frontier on the left, then you'd spot the Desert Inn on the right and the El Rancho on the left, and finally you'd see the Thunderbird on the right. That was it.

At that time, a major draw at these hotels was the food. Each hotel casino laid on a complimentary twenty-four-hour buffet. Gambler or not, you could eat for free in Las Vegas at those five hotels on the strip. Another big attraction was the girls (and to say "girls" was perfectly okay back then). Each hotel had a chorus line of at least sixteen girls, and each understood her obligation to mix with the customers between shows. Las Vegas got its original reputation as a den of iniquity from the many girls who willingly provided sexual favors, especially to the guys who gambled with hundred-dollar chips. If that still goes on—and it probably does—the chips are worth more like a thousand dollars.

I should say that not all chorus girls fell into this category. Many were well educated, from so-called good families, and they were there because they loved theater and show business. But they, too, understood that they had to "mix" between shows. They were smart enough to pull it off without getting into anything they didn't want to get into.

Having said that, whenever I'm invited to speak, I open with the words, "They say that show business is all about parties every night, naked women, sex, drugs, and booze. And it's true—I wouldn't be in any other business!" This gets a laugh, but it really isn't true. In the course of my showbiz life, I haven't seen anything to justify that cliché. In terms of desperation, degradation, drug and alcohol abuse, sexual promiscuity, or whatever else show business's detractors want to throw in, Hollywood is not that different from any metropolitan city in the United States. I have traveled widely and seen it all, and I can say, with certainty, that if you want kinky, you can get it anywhere. Hollywood has no exclusive on kinky.

The tabloid stories about the stars are essentially ridiculous. It wouldn't surprise me if one of those rags proclaimed that President Bush had sex with his rocking horse when he was three years old. Some stars choose to ignore this kind of reporting—not wanting to dignify it with a response—but others—Carol Burnett and, more recently, Clint Eastwood, Tom Cruise, and Cindy Crawford—have opted to sue the tabloids for printing blatant lies about them.

While it's not easy being famous, I can honestly say that the actors I've dealt with over the years are no different from you or your neighbor. They harbor the same emotions, they laugh about the same things, they experience the same heartbreaks and woulda-coulda-shoulda frustrations. Some are religious, some are not; some are honest, some dishonest, some hardworking, some lazy—and on it goes. Drug and alcohol problems drag down some; others escape that fate. Some have psychological problems; some keep it together. Some have relationship dilemmas; others live quietly with their mates. Stars may have a lot more money than the average person, but many acquire it far too fast and find themselves unable to handle it. They are the ones who wind up broke.

Stars live under a spotlight that magnifies their assets and liabilities, and sometimes it blinds them and those who watch them. One thing that most people don't seem to realize is how vulnerable and uncertain many performers are, even those who have reached the top. I remember when Dean Martin and Jerry Lewis broke up, and Dean was set to do his first solo club date. I sat with him beforehand in his dressing room. "How does it feel being on your own?" I asked him casually, not expecting the answer I got. "I'm scared— really scared," he said. Then I looked closely at him and, yes, I could see it in his face.

Something similar happened to Sammy Davis Junior. Before he got to be as big as Jack Benny, I booked him at the Shrine Auditorium as a prelude to booking him at Ciro's. When you made it to Ciro's, you were in. Well, Sammy ripped that Shrine Auditorium audience to shreds. They were on their feet screaming and clapping. I thought the place would come down. He walked off the stage and said to me, very seriously, "How did I do?"

Recalling my experiences with the business end of showbiz, I think about the days when I only had to talk to one guy if I wanted to sell a TV show to a network. Today, you have to deal with thirty people before any decision is reached. And it was the same in movies—you talked to the top guys: Harry Cohn, Darryl Zanuck, Dore Schary. The decisions were theirs alone.

I also can't help being concerned about the ways broadcast news reporting has changed over the years. Today much of it's just simplistic sound bytes leveled at the broadest possible audience. The attention span of today's TV audience is very small and, consequently, news is quickly read from a teleprompter without any analysis or comment. James Brooks's movie *Broadcast News* did a great job of mocking the whole thing. It seems we've turned into a nation of impatient, clicker-happy fools, unwilling to sit still for any piece of information that doesn't make a direct and instantaneous connection to our brains—preferably to its pleasure center. TV shows like *Hard Copy* and *A Current Affair* jazz up news items just enough to keep us watching; few people care anymore whether the stories are sensationalized or distorted or even downright false. "What's the difference?" viewers reason. "We can't do anything about it anyway."

I'm also shocked when I think about how the cost of doing business has skyrocketed. Today, the costs for making a record, a movie, a TV pilot, a special, or a Broadway play are astronomical. In an effort to survive, some megacorporations in the theater business are merging or buying each other out. Every day you hear about another: Warner Brothers and Ted Turner, ABC and Disney, Universal and Seagram, Viacom and Paramount, General Electric and NBC, Columbia and Sony.

Some good changes have taken place, however, and we shouldn't gloss over them. In my early days in Hollywood, for example, people referred to Rock Hudson as a "queer." That kind of thing doesn't happen today. In Hollywood, as in most other places, few people care too much about an individual's sexual preferences. Overall, there's more of a live-and-let-live attitude now; but just compare that to the attitude that prevailed back in the forties and fifties. There's a remarkable difference.

It's similar to the problems once faced by black stars, which I talked about earlier. When I was working in Las Vegas and Reno and Tahoe, Harry Belafonte and Lena Horne and other black stars of the era had to enter the hotels and nightclubs they were performing in by the back doors. Today, black stars like Cuba Gooding, Morgan Freeman, Danny Glover, Lou Gossett, Eddie Murphy, Wesley Snipes, Denzel Washington, Samuel L. Jackson, and Will Smith—and Hispanic stars such as Edward James Olmos and Jimmy Smits—are working as actors and directors.

In addition, strong black voices, like Spike Lee, John Singleton, and the Wayans brothers, are breaking new ground with their films. Just imagine: at one time, the only TV show featuring blacks was *Amos 'n' Andy*. Then Bill Cosby came along, and now, multitalented women like Oprah Winfrey and Whoopi Goldberg are taking the next step. Both own their own production companies (Harpo for Oprah, and One Ho Productions for Whoopi).

I am thrilled to have found a major talent in Dan Gasby, and we have plans to work together. We intend to take classic theater pieces and books that are in the public domain and use them as vehicles for actors, writers, directors, producers, and editors representing diverse races and ethnic backgrounds. Bringing our different backgrounds and sensibilities to the job—I'm white, he's African American—we're looking forward to an exciting collaboration.

So, as the world turns, so does show business. The art that this business produces—like all art—reflects what our values are at any given point in time and illuminates the mores of our society. It helps us to understand, at a gut level, that we are not alone in our craziness, our hopes, and our follies, that we all have darker sides that we don't like to own up to. These days, it's a cliché to say that theater makes us laugh and cry and own up to the best and worst of being human, but clichés get to be clichés because there's a truth in them that doesn't diminish with time.

Anyone in show business is aware of the frequent refrain coming from the wannabes: "I could do that," they insist as they watch Jay Leno, Kevin Costner, Tom Cruise, or Madonna. And many of these aspirants actually have the talent they need to make it. But it's guts, tenacity, and drive that assure success, whether your aim is to be a singer, dancer, actor, writer, director, or producer. The ability to take an emotional beating and stick to it without losing your faith and resolve is what will bring you success.

Show me any big star, and I'll show you a person who withstood overwhelming rejection at the beginning of his or her career. Being turned down, passed over, and told you have no talent is a common experience; you hear it from both diehards and dropouts. The theater business is something like baseball. If you're a three-hundred hitter, it means that every ten times you go to bat you're going to flop seven times and win three times. Very few theater people bat three hundred. They're more like one-hundred hitters. We always gear ourselves for perfection, knowing that there's a seventy-percent chance of failure. But you've got to start out with the idea of perfection. (And sometimes a perfect act is based on its planned imperfection. When I was with Sha Na Na, the guys always danced a little out of step. That's what made the act work.)

In other words, you have to realize that you'll have your ups and downs. The ups teach you about the downs, and the downs teach you about the ups. It's kind of a universal law—philosophers, the old and revered as well as a host of present-day gurus, keep reminding us about it. And it's true. But I learned it from my own life experience, not from anything I ever read or studied.

Is there a system to show biz? Yes. Can I explain it? No. The one thing that remains at a premium is talent—and the people who have it. The other players—the studio heads, managers, agents, publicists, attorneys, accountants, equipment handlers, those who operate the delivery systems that support the industry—all depend on talent. Today, multimedia has launched a talent feeding frenzy; with the globalization of cable and satellite technology, the talent search is like the whale's search for the plankton it needs to satisfy its voracious appetite.

A major problem today is that people with a minimum of talent are being allowed to take over starring roles. With a good "look" and a good "attitude," you can get yourself a good part. Before the current frenzy, only real talent could do that. But in the production end of the business—my end of it—it's still true that only those who have strong theatrical perception and imagination can enter the world of the rich and famous. I'm sure that this will remain true in the decades to come.

And let me say something about that kind of perception. I see theater everywhere. It doesn't just happen on a stage or a set. You'll see theater in a Catholic church at high mass. A doctor who has a good bedside manner is using theater to make people well. There's theater in certain business enterprises. I once went into a supermarket in Finland, and the way they had stacked the shelves with cans and bottles and packages was something to behold: I felt like I was in the Museum of Modern Art.

You see theater in education too. Most professors have enough knowledge of their fields to teach their students what they need to know. But the professor who mounts a lecture in a theatrical way is the one the students remember, the one who inspires them down the road. The late physicist Richard Feynman was a superb showman, as is biologist Richard Eakin. Now professor emeritus, in the sixties and seventies Eakin would actually deliver his lectures dressed as famous scientists from times past. In other words, I'm not just talking about professors of literature and the dramatic arts.

And then there are the star-quality performers who don't want anything to do with my world. I remember well hearing a recording of gospel music that included songs by a young woman named Eva Thornquist. I thought she was fantastic, so I tracked her down. She was working in Phoenix in one of those revival-meeting tents, so off I went to Arizona. When I heard Eva in person, I didn't have a single doubt: this girl could be big. I caught up with her after the show. She was selling records and bibles at a side table. I introduced myself and started telling her how much she could do for her church when she became a giant superstar, and I was the one who could make it happen. I told her, "Eight weeks from now, right in the middle of the Grammy Awards show, a young girl will walk from the back of the theater, through the audience of 6,500 people, singing her heart out. By the time she gets onto the stage, everyone will know that Eva Thornquist is the world's best new singer. And that's just the first step; that's a drop in the bucket to where we'll go from there. Pretty soon, you'll have sixty million people listening to that voice of yours."

Somehow, Eva Thornquist decided that all of this glory would take away from her service to God. I had half a mind to tell her, "God's got you playing Phoenix." But I thought better of it. Nothing I could say would sway Eva or her husband.

What disturbs me most about show business today is that it's turned into a huge numbers game. It's a far cry from what it was during my first fifteen years. Then, the industry was still relatively small, and everyone knew everyone else. It was one big fraternity. The guy selling acts and bands sat next to the guy selling movies and TV, and he sat next to the guy booking concert tours. Each network or studio assigned only one person to deal with us, and we all had a handshake relationship with that person. The record people, the motion picture people, the variety people, and the Broadway people all knew each other. Gone are the days of the Brown Derby restaurant and its constant ebb and flow of showbiz people. And gone are the breakfasts at the Beverly Hills Hotel, where people in the business, who knew each other intimately, would meet and talk.

These days, faceless monsters parade around town armed with a long list of executive titles. It sometimes seems as if we have more cogs than wheels in Hollywood. Maybe this has been good for the industry's bottom line, but for those in my age group—ask any of them—it's not nearly as much fun as it once was.

Showbiz has taught me a lot, and I still hold some of the same opinions I formed years ago. About Broadway, for example: my Will Rogers experience made it very clear to me that a new system to mount Broadway shows has to be developed. Broadway desperately needs to come up with incentives to bring in investors willing to underwrite theatrical productions and build new theaters. Even now, I am hard at work with some heavyweight investment bankers to accomplish just that.

Thirty-one years ago, I dreamed of building the Grammy Awards into a show that would air live around the world. My dream has yet to be realized, although the Latin Grammy Awards show, which got started in 2000, represents a major move in that direction. We were picked up live in over two hundred countries. Another dream I had was to produce the Grammys from Madison Square Garden. I'd tried on different occasions to get the Recording Academy to agree to do the show from the Sports Arena in Los Angeles or the Los Angeles Forum, but I was voted down. When, after a long fight, I finally got the green light to produce the show from Madison Square Garden, I was under the severest pressure I had ever faced. There was barely a person who agreed with me that this previously intimate show could be staged in front of an arena crowd of fourteen thousand. But it was a huge success, and after the show I felt like I could fly over the city of New York without a plane, helicopter, or parachute. Victory at last!

My next scheme is to do the show from the Rose Bowl or Yankee Stadium. I can hear the objections now, but it will come to pass, and it will be sensational.

I recently read something that Picasso apparently said: "Every child is an artist. The problem is how to remain an artist once one grows up." I believe that, and it has motivated me to start planning a summer camp for inner-city kids. The idea is to provide kids with the opportunity to explore their innate talents. There will be instruction in voice, acting, comedy, and writing. When it's time for the campers to head home, each will be given a videotape of his or her individual accomplishments—whether it be acting in a play, singing a song, or doing a stand-up comedy routine; the writers will have tapes of sketches they've written, performed by others.

Some of my friends wonder why I don't take vacations the way they do. The only bona fide vacations I've ever taken are the two trips to Europe—with Foopie before she died, and with Five before we married. Our place in Canada is an ideal spot for what most people think of as R&R, but the truth is that I consider my entire life to have been a vacation. I have no urge to travel to foreign lands and spend my time lining up to see a statue or a tree or a famous whatever.

When all is said and done, the best vacation I can imagine is sitting at my desk watching the phones light up, promising me another day in show business.

Afterword

AS I LOOK BACK OVER what I've written, I see that I've given the impression that it's all been a one-man show. This disturbs me, because it's far from the truth. Show business is an extremely collaborative venture. It takes a team to pull off a successful show—be it a movie, a concert, a record, or a television special. If I expressed my thanks to everyone who deserved it, their names would fill another book, so I'll confine my thank-yous here to those involved with the Grammy Awards. First, I thank the past presidents:

N.A.R.A.S. Past Presidents

1969-71	Irving Townsend
1971-73	Wesley H. Rose
1973-75	Bill Lowery
1975-77	Jay L. Cooper
1977-79	J. William Denny
1979-81	Jay S. Lowy
1981-83	William Ivey

1983-85	Michael Melvoin
1985-87	Michael Greene
1987-89	Alfred Schlesinger
1989-91	William Ivey
1991-93	Ron Kramer
1993-95	Henry L. Neuberger III
1995-97	Joel A. Katz
1997-99	Phil Ramone
1999-2000	Leslie Ann Jones
2000-02	Garth Fundis

I would also like to thank all members of the Television Committees and the Recording Academy in general, including: Murray Allen, sound designer; Christine Clark Bradley, associate director; John Bradley, staging supervisor; Bob Dickinson, lighting designer; Andrea Dossa, associate producer; Ken Erlich, producer/writer; Jack Elliott, music director; Tisha Fein, talent executive; John Field, technical director; Ed Greene, audio; Richard Harris, attorney; Bob Henry, producer/director; Robert Keene, production designer; Paul Keyes, producer; Buzz Kohan, writer; Walter Miller, producer/director; Marty Pasetta, producer/director; Bob Precht, producer; Sharon Taylor, package producer/tape A.D; and personal assistants Josie Speight, Carolyn Machado, and Gloria Dimine.

Appendix

Some of the stars who have appeared in Cossette Productions:

Aerosmith

Christina Aguilera

Ann-Margret

Roseanne Arnold

Aykroyd, Dan

Babyface

Burt Bacharach

Backstreet Boys

Lucille Ball

Antonio Banderas

Jack Benny

Leonard Bernstein

Valerie Bertinelli

Andre Bocelli

Boyz II Men

Garth Brooks

Carol Burnett

Michael Caine

Mariah Carey

Johnny Cash

Tracy Chapman

Ray Charles

Chevy Chase

Eric Clapton

Natalie Cole

Harry Connick, Jr.

Bill Cosby

Crosby, Stills & Nash

Billy Crystal

Rodney Dangerfield

Ellen DeGeneres

Oscar De La Hoya

John Denver

Danny Devito

Neil Diamond

Céline Dion

Placido Domingo

Kirk Douglas

Faye Dunaway

Clint Eastwood

Gloria Estefan

Melissa Etheridge

Peter Falk

Sally Field

Jane Fonda

Aretha Franklin

Peter Gabriel

James Galway

James Garner

Vince Gill

Richard Gere

Jackie Gleason

Whoopi Goldberg

Kelsey Grammer

Amy Grant

Herbie Hancock

Valerie Harper

Goldie Hawn

Hootie & The Blowfish

Bob Hope

Lena Horn

Whitney Houston

Billy Joel

Olivia Newton-John

Quincy Jones

B.B. King

Kris Kristofferson

LL Cool J

kd lang

Angela Lansbury

Michele Lee

Annie Lennox

Jay Leno

Shelly Long

Jennifer Lopez

Shirley MacLaine

Madonna

Ricky Martin

Steve Martin

Lee Marvin

Johnny Mathis

Walter Matthau

Paul McCartney

Bobby McFerrin

Bette Midler

Liza Minnelli

Mary Tyler Moore

Alanis Morissette

Eddie Murphy

*NSYNC

Willie Nelson

Aaron Neville

Bob Newhart

Olivia Newton-John

Jack Nicholson

Rosie O'Donnell

Luciano Pavarotti

Gregory Peck

Itzhak Perlman

Bernadette Peters

Sidney Poitier

Richard Pryor

Bonnie Raitt

Paul Reiser

Burt Reynolds

Don Rickles

Kenny Rogers

Linda Ronstadt

Santana

Telly Savalas

Ricky Schroder

Arnold Schwarzenegger

Seal

Bob Segar

Tom Selleck

Shakira

Garry Shandling

Brook Shields

Paul Simon

Frank Sinatra

Will Smith

Britney Spears

Bruce Springsteen

Sylvester Stallone

Jean Stapleton

Ringo Starr

Sting

Meryl Streep

Barbra Streisand

Marty Stuart

Patrick Swayze

Lily Tomlin

Travis Tritt

Luther Vandross

Dick Van Dyke

Raquel Welch

Andy Williams

Vanessa Williams

Stevie Wonder

Trisha Yearwood

Dwight Yoakam